Cover Image Credit/Copyright Attribution: IIIerlok_Xolms/Shutterstock

Interventions in Digital Cultures

Digital Cultures Series

Edited by Andreas Bernard, Armin Beverungen, Irina Kaldrack,
Martina Leeker, Sascha Simons and Florian Sprenger

A book series of the *Digital Cultures Research Lab*

Interventions in Digital Cultures: Technology, the Political, Methods

edited by

Howard Caygill, Martina Leeker and Tobias Schulze

**Bibliographical Information of the
German National Library**
The German National Library lists this publication in the
Deutsche Nationalbibliografie (German National Bib-
liography); detailed bibliographic information is available
online at http://dnb.d-nb.de.

Contents

INFRASTRUCTURES

RESILIENCE

PERFORMATIVITY

AMBIVALENCES

CRITIQUE

Introduction: Interventions in Digital Cultures

**Martina Leeker, Tobias Schulze
and Howard Caygill**

Focusing Ambivalences of Interventions in Digital Cultures

This volume intends to outline and analyze interventions, under the specific conditions of digital cultures, as theory and practice of critique; political action (for example protest, demonstration, or occupation), and public spheres (politische Öffentlichkeit). Interventions are understood as activities that engage in social and political contexts, often with artistic means, hoping to interrupt critical situations and ultimately change social, economic, or technological conditions. Activist applications of interventions eclipse the managerial and military sense of interventions related to war, oppression, and control; the focus is on applications that represent the positively valued emancipatory efforts of self-organized, collective, subversive intervention by political, activist and artistic communities, among others.

The premise of this volume is that interventions are influenced and shaped by the conditions and epistemologies of digital cultures, even when not directly technological. Exploring the possibilities of participating and intervening in digital cultures requires a prior analysis of the cultures themselves, for such interventions happen within zones of infrastructures that are not fully visible, understandable, or controllable. The task is no less than to intervene in the socio-technological and techno-political conditions of existence that lie beyond our consciousness and appear to be out of our hands. As technological environments and concepts are understood as ubiquitous, we cannot escape them, so interventions always have to reckon with them. In order to intervene effectively in such environments and conceptual structures we must be able to analyze them and, if necessary, adapt to them. This predicament of being shaped and shaping becomes constitutive for intervention. It is against this background that the book asks how interventions are shaped by the conditions of digital cultures, and how they can contribute reflexively to altering and reshaping these conditions.

Engaging with these questions and situations, the book adopts a twofold approach. The first involves studying interventions and focuses on the reciprocal shaping and reshaping of digital cultures and interventions. A deeper understanding of the constitution of interventions in digital cultures is required, because it may be that not every aesthetic of interventions is able to interrupt digitality. Could interventions unwillingly repeat the constitutive conditions that they intend to intervene in? This problematic situation leads to the second approach, which follows the conditions of interventions in digital cultures and explores, furthermore, their proper constitution, concerning, for example, their genealogy (Fred Turner's contribution), their involvement in the history and constitution of the political (Howard Caygill's contribution), their entanglement with the sometimes ideological constitution of technology (Wendy Hui Kyong Chun's contribution), gender aspects (Kat Jungnickel and Ulrike Bergermann's contributions), and the politics of space (Ulrike Bergermann's contribution).

With these contributions, the volume aims to intervene reflexively and critically in the field of interventions through a close reading of their conditions, genealogies, constitutions, and entanglements, and hence their hidden political sense and regime.

Challenges of Interventions Under the Conditions of Digital Cultures

It is remarkable that interventions have been in vogue (Hartmann, Lemke, and Nitsche 2012) since the 2000s as "the" form of critique, political action, and public spheres (politische Öffentlichkeit) in digital cultures. In 2012, Friedrich von Borries, professor and curator of design at the Academy of Art in Hamburg, published a glossary of interventions subtitled: "Approximations towards a too-much-used, but too-little-defined notion" (von Borries et al. 2012).[1] Borries maintains that: "Interventions are the miracle cure of our times. Quickly in, intervening, quickly out. Great effect—little effort. In war, in the arts, in urban development, in therapy"[2]. This estimation also holds for the aesthetics of contemporary interventions with artistic means or in activist contexts, which focus on performative approaches (Klein [2012] 2013). They tend to make intervening an end in itself, establishing acting as a recursive system. Interventions are always ready for the next action; they are self-referential, performing for a potential future and coming up with not a new order but the next intervention, pointing to a further intervention. The question is whether and how this hype is related to digital cultures.

---

1   German title: *Glossar der Interventionen: Annäherung an einen überverwendeten, aber unterbestimmten Begriff*.

2   "Interventionen sind das Wundermittel unserer Zeit. Schnell rein, eingreifen, schnell raus. Große Wirkung mit wenig Aufwand. Im Krieg, in der Kunst, in der Stadtentwicklung, im therapeutischen Bereich" (von Borries 2012, verso). English translation by the authors.

14   It is striking that in a situation where digital cultures become
performative (Leeker, Schipper, and Beyes 2016) and unleash
automation and self-organizing infrastructures, interventions are
really hyping performative manners of acting and protest (Klein
2017). While technological devices become agents themselves,
generating reality and engaging with human agents in affective
(Angerer 2015) techno-social ensembles (Sprenger and Engemann
2015), interventions invented themselves as a performative
force, and engage in social change just by performing. While
globally networked infrastructures fall into a continuous and
self-reliant processing of data, intervention emerges as the
engendering, even the installing, of a regime of endless processes
of intervening.

This logic opens a comparison to what Orit Halpern (2017) as well
as Halpern and Robert Mitchell (2017) call the "smart mandate" of
infrastructures in digital cultures. This mandate points to a further aspect according to the actual insights of research on digital
cultures. It is not just about a regime of infrastructures that are
invisible to human agents and operate beyond human consciousness, collecting and processing data for profiling and predicting
future activities. Nor is it purely about subjects being constituted
and controlled, as Antoinette Rouvroy (2013) explains, by "data-
behavior" and an "algorithmic governmentality." It is particularly
to do with a culture of distributed, worldwide, smart infrastructures that comes up with an epistemology of uncertainty
and resilience. Resilience is constituted by the idea and practice
that reality is too complex to be controlled or predicted and that
the self-organized infrastructures should be capable of resisting
and surviving political or ecological attacks by virtue of their own
capacities and organization. In this epistemology of resilience,
socio-technological existence becomes, according to Halpern and
Mitchell, a permanent demonstration or test for the adaptation
of the next unpredictable event. This demo-regime announces
the end of the socio-political task of problem solving. There are
no problems, only affordances for the optimization of resilient

adaptation. This regime of smartness corresponds interestingly
with the hype of performative interventions mentioned above.
Both deny solutions and instead perform interventions—the pure
and continuous testing and experimenting of resilience.

The epistemological similarity between the hyped performative
aesthetics of interventions and the infrastructural environment
reminds us that the constitution of interventions takes place
according to the technological conditions of digital cultures. They
are then not just intervening in, but perpetuating, digital cultures,
supporting them and generating a kind of digital impotence via
interventions. People become hyper-occupied with intervening
the moment they are asked to perform as data providers in
accordance with the technological and economic needs and interests of digital cultures. Intervening with performative aesthetics
means feeding, unwillingly, the whole-earth-data-network with
performances of itself. In this ambivalent situation, we need to
investigate whether the interventions that constitute our capacity
to reflect and act, and even our ability to resist, are not inex-
tricably entangled in the conditions that we want to intervene in.

Intervening and the Constitution of Interventions

A critical and reflexive use of interventions must be envisaged
to avoid the unwilling repetition of those regimes of digital
cultures. This book proposes a twofold method to establish such
usage—combining analysis of digital cultures and the role of
interventions in them with systematic exploration of the constitution of interventions. It could be realized by reconstructing
genealogies of interventions or by rethinking the concepts and
discourses of interventions—an integral element of the contributions to this volume. Another option would be to carefully
revise intervention methods by comparing them with the techno-
epistemological impacts of digital cultures.

16   What is revealed is that interventions with artistic means can be part of a politic of forced democratization, as in the Cold War (Fred Turner's contribution), as well as an instrument of resistance in war and revolution (Howard Caygill's contribution). Following the twofold analysis can inform us about intervention methods, showing that pure interruption has become senseless in digital cultures, as it is part of digital recursion. Suddenly, it is the establishment of sustainable, alternative structures and technologies (Alexander R. Galloway and Wendy Hui Kyong Chun's contributions) that becomes the perfect and adequate intervention.

Interventions should be accepted and taken seriously in their ambivalence and doubleness. Interventions are highly relative, driven by theories and discourses on their constitution. Interventions may therefore look completely different according to the theoretical insights in which they are couched. Interventions are not a priori "good" in the sense of emancipatory potentials and effects. Their constitution means that interventions can be included in regulation and control, and they can be engaged for social change, making themselves obsolete, as Steve Kurtz points out in his interview, once the structures and dominance relationships that are the target of interventions have been dismantled.

Outline of the Book

To undertake the explorations needed, this volume brings together scholars from philosophy, political theory, media studies, and sociology/ethnology as well as practitioners of interventions. Their texts unfold to reveal an assemblage of diverse intervention methods. Beyond the perspectives of single disciplines or specific aesthetic approaches to interventions, methods can be seen as the common ground of the different contributions. Each considers a specific aspect of intervention in digital cultures and develops from it a critical and practical engagement. It is hoped that this interplay of methods and their

theoretical foundation will support a productive thinking, which   **17**
is inspired by the ambivalences of interventions, and lend the
volume relevance as a critical and practical guide for future
interventions.

Acknowledgements

This volume originated from the symposium *Technological Conditions of Interventions: History, Epistemology, Dramaturgy*, held in May 2015 at the Digital Cultures Research Lab (DCRL) of Leuphana University.[3] We are very thankful to the symposium participants (Ulrike Bergermann, David Berry, Howard Caygill, Hervé Fischer, Bernard Dionysius Geoghegan, Kat Jungnickel, Marcell Mars, Alexandre Monnin, Imanuel Schipper, Fred Turner, and Nina Wakeford) for their valuable and inspiring talks and vivid discussions, as well as, of course, for the individual contributors' essays for this volume that arose from the symposium. The book also contains interviews with scholars who play an important role in the research and practice of interventions: they enrich the volume enormously, referring to the conditions of interventions in digital cultures, and we are thus very grateful to the interviewees we were able to lure into participating.

This book itself wouldn't be as it is if it weren't for the helpful and professional aides and assistants. A big thank you goes out to Inga Luchs for her work on typesetting and formatting the manuscript, to Janet Leyton-Grant for her patient and accurate proofreading, and to Sara Morais for the transcription of interview material. Moreover, we want to express our gratitude to the editorial board for cooperative and important critical reviews. Finally, we are indebted to and want to thank Ina Dubberke, Samantha Gupta, Irina Kaldrack, and Armin Beverungen for their support and paramount organizing talent, for both the symposium and the publication; their commitment, and that of

---

3   For documentation of symposium contributions, see Leeker 2015.

 our DCRL colleagues, affords us the opportunity for truly transdisciplinary scholarship, discussions, and academic exchange.

References

Angerer, Marie-Luise. 2015. *Desire After Affect.* London/New York: Rowman and
Littlefield.

Halpern, Orit. 2017. "Hopeful Resilience, Efflux, Architectures." Accessed
May 10, 2017. http://www.e-flux.com/architecture/accumulation/96421/
hopeful-resilience/.

Halpern, Orit, and Robert Mitchell. 2017 (forthcoming). "The Smartness Mandate:
Notes Toward a Critique." In *Grey Room.* Accessed March 29, 2017.
https://static1.squarespace.com/static/53c7f8cce4b0e4db83a38f5b/t/58752be7
20099e802621da15/1484073960267/smartnessmandate+Halpern.pdf.

Hartmann, Doreen, Inga Lemke, and Jessica Nitsche, eds. 2012. *Interventionen:
Grenzüberschreitungen in Ästhetik, Politik und Ökonomie.* Munich: Fink.

Klein, Gabriele. (2012) 2013. "Choreografien des Alltags: Bewegung und Tanz im
Kontext Kultureller Bildung." Kulturelle Bildung Online. Accessed March 29, 2017.
https://www.kubi-online.de/artikel/choreografien-des-alltags-bewegung-tanz-
kontext-kultureller-bildung.

Klein, Gabriele. 2017. "Urban Choreographies: Artistic Intervention and the Politics
of Urban Space." In *The Oxford Handbook of Dance and Politics*, edited by Rebekah
Kowal, Randy Martin, and Gerald Siegmund, 131–148. New York: Oxford University Press.

Leeker, Martina. 2015. "Technological Conditions of Interventions: History, Epistemology, Dramaturgy." Experiments&Interventions. Accessed March 29, 2017.
http://projects.digital-cultures.net/dcrl-experiments-interventions/
politische-oekonomie/interventions/.

Leeker, Martina, Imanuel Schipper, and Timon Beyes, eds. 2016. *Performing the
Digital: Performativity and Performance Studies in Digital Cultures.* Bielefeld:
transcript.

Rouvroy, Antoinette. 2013. "The End(s) of Critique: Data-Behaviourism vs. Due-
Process." In *Privacy, Due Process and the Computational Turn: Philosophers of Law
Meet Philosophers of Technology*, edited by Mireille Hildebrandt and Katja de Vries,
143–168. Abingdon: Routledge.

Sprenger, Florian and Christoph Engemann, eds. 2015. *Internet der Dinge: Über
smarte Objekte, intelligente Umgebungen und die technische Durchdringung der
Welt.* Bielefeld: transcript.

von Borries, Friedrich, Christian Hiller, Daniel Kerber, Friederike Wegner, and
Anna-Lena Wenzel. 2012. *Glossar der Interventionen: Annäherung an einen
überverwendeten, aber unterbestimmten Begriff (IMD).* Berlin: Merve.

MULTIMEDIA

DEMOCRACY

SURROUND

DEMOCRATIC PERSONALITY

FASCISM

1

Surrounds, Be-Ins, and Performative Participation: Shady Sides of Art and Interventions

**An Interview with Fred Turner
by Martina Leeker**

Beginning in the 1940s, a group of former Bauhaus designers, American artists, and American intellectuals sought to intervene in cultural and political transformations. To revisit that history is to see how art and political power can become entwined, even when artists have the most democratic of intentions. In the 1940s, Americans built multimedia environments—democratic surrounds—which they hoped would help generate liberal democratic personalities by training audiences to curate their own aesthetic experiences. In the 1960s, these environments gave rise to an artistically grounded psychedelic Be-In and to a new holistic participation in a world

of electronic media. In both cases, however, designers, scientists, artists, and politicians hoped that media would become both a means of liberation and a mode of control. This history leaves us with the question of which aesthetics and art forms could support a more democratic mode of engagement today. By working through the history of interventions and the arts, this conversation aims to reveal lures and traps that should be avoided in contemporary interventions.

Martina Leeker: Nowadays, we see hype around artistic interventions as well as about art as intervention, both being considered practices to generate and develop a public sphere and the self-determined capacity to act. But we learn from the research in your books, *From Counterculture to Cyberculture* (Turner 2006) and *The Democratic Surround* (Turner 2013a), that art is not a priori "good," in the sense that it is not per se democratizing, bringing more capacity to act, to resist, or to change conditions for people. Thus, before doing interventions with artistic means or art as intervention, it is important to do a historical checkup concerning the politics of interventionist artwork since the 1940s.

Fred Turner: The books together trace a history of the intersection of art, counterculture, and technology from about 1940 in the US to when the Internet goes public, which is about 1993. It's about a 50-year arc. What you see in that period is a constant back and forth between the art world and the technology world. They're not separate; there is a very similar class of people working in both spaces and there are a whole series of spaces where they intersect with each other.

During World War II, artists began to develop multi-image environments and a really rich environmental sensibility. It went on to have a big impact on how we thought about computing later. But in the 1940s it was pre-digital. It was a way of trying to make a really democratic medium. At the time, many Americans believed that one-to-many media such as film, cinema, newspapers, and radio reflected a top-down, authoritarian mind-set. A certain set of artists and propagandists wanted to build a surround. They wanted every individual to be surrounded by images or sounds so they could be free to choose what they wanted from that environment. That idea migrated into the technical world through Margaret Mead and Gregory Bateson (Turner 2013a), who were involved in both wartime propaganda efforts and were central participants in the Macy Conferences[1] that brought us cybernetics. By the late 1940s, when Norbert Wiener was working on cybernetics, he was thinking both technically and with models of environmental communication that actually come from Bauhaus refugees to American propaganda, and from there, through Mead and Bateson, to cybernetics.

And that's just the first of many kinds of intersection points. Later, during the 1960s, Billy Klüver's[2] group, Experiments in Art and Technology (E.A.T.), brought engineers from the Bell Telephone Laboratories (Bell Labs) together with painters and performance artists in New York. Even before

---

1   The interdisciplinary Macy Conferences were held from 1941 to 1960 in New York, within the cybernetic conferences from 1946 to 1953. (Pias 2003)

2   Billy Klüver was an engineer at Bell Labs. He founded Experiments in Art and Technology with artist Robert Rauschenberg in 1967. Klüver started to collaborate with artists such as Jean Tinguely at the beginning of the 1960s. His aim for engaging in the collaboration of engineers and artists was to make technology more human.

that, people like the architect, systems theorist, designer, and inventor Buckminster Fuller were bridges between the worlds. Buckminster Fuller patented the geodesic dome in 1952 and sold it to the American military to house radar for the Defense Early Warning Line, the DEW-line. It then became the preferred housing of back-to-the-land commune builders in the 1960s and early 1970s. So, it's a kind of back and forth between the arts and technology. And I think that's what we're seeing in many art worlds today.

ML: What is the socio-cultural, the political and the epistemological impact of this back and forth of art and technology, even military, and what are the kind of problems it brings for combining art and interventions?

FT: In the late 1930s and early 1940s, American sociologists, social thinkers, psychologists, anthropologists, and political leaders were all students of what was called at the time "culture and personality anthropology." They believed that every culture had a kind of dominant, modal personality and that families trained children to match that personality. So, people thought, for example, that Germans had a kind of authoritarian personality style and that somehow Hitler had latched on to that. People also believed that media, meaning movies, radio and the like, were like extensions of the family. After you grew up and left home, media did the work of continuing to form your subjectivity in ways that were appropriate to your culture. Thus, they believed that German media would need to be more authoritarian, while American media were meant to be more democratic.

And this was partly how Americans explained to themselves the mystery of Adolf Hitler. Until the late 1930s, Americans really believed that Germany represented the pinnacle of European culture. When Hitler became chancellor in Germany, Americans were just mystified. How had the most cultured nation in Europe turned to this guy for leadership?

One of the most popular answers was that somehow Hitler had mastered the mass media. He had somehow built a kind of mediated system for taking Germans away from their rational cultured selves and just melting them into an authoritarian mass.

As World War II got under way, American leaders thought to themselves, "Okay, look, we need to have morale, like the Germans have. We need to be as strong as the Germans. But we can't make our citizens into authoritarians." So, there was a big debate in the Roosevelt administration. One side said, "Joseph Goebbels, he's doing great. We should do what he does and if our citizens become authoritarians, too bad. We'll fix that later." It's terrifying, but that was a real discussion. And then there was another side, and it was led by a group called the Committee for National Morale, which Margaret Mead and Gregory Bateson were part of. This side said, "Now look, we need to find a democratic kind of morale, and we need to build a media form that will sustain it." They theorized democratic morale using a mix of democracy theory and personality theory. A democratic person, they said, was someone who could choose their own experience, who had a uniquely integrated set of experiences, who could embrace others who were very different than themselves, across racial lines, across lines of sexual preference, across national lines—in other words, a cultured, cosmopolitan liberal. That person had to be made. And they believed that the best way to make them with media was to surround them with images or sounds from which people could choose the elements that were most meaningful to them. As they chose those things, they would be practicing the styles of perception on which the democratic personality depended.

The members of the Committee for National Morale didn't actually make media. But in 1942, at the Museum of Modern Art (MoMA) in New York, their ideas became the basis of a propaganda exhibition called "Road to Victory."

It was designed by Herbert Bayer, a Bauhaus figure who had recently immigrated to the United States, together with Edward Steichen, the photographer who would go on to create, from 1951 till its opening of 1955, what almost certainly remains the most widely seen photography exhibition of all time: "The Family of Man." "Road to Victory" was an image environment with pictures of America hung over people's heads, down by their feet, at every level. People were meant to walk through it together, yet have unique, individualized experiences, to choose what they wanted to see and to see it in their own way. They were meant to be individuals together—that's the liberal ideal, that's the American ideal in that period, that's the democratic mode of morale. Bayer and Steichen hoped that by creating these surrounds, they would give people the "freedom" to define themselves as individuals and as citizens, simultaneously.

Now of course from our own time we can see that these surrounds are *surrounds*—people have choices, but the choices have been set for them ahead of time. They can only choose among the images that are there. They can only choose among the perceptions that are available to them in a setting that's been curated. I would argue that that's a lot like our media environment today. We have lots and lots of choices but all of them carefully curated.

ML: This means that we can't thoughtlessly take the aesthetic dispositive of surrounding people with multi-optional media environments as a method of intervention today because it is based on a problematic understanding of democracy. It is about a kind of elitist curating; some people know what is good for mankind better than others. So, we have to make do with an ambivalent aesthetic-political endeavor because on the one hand it trains decision making and individuality and on the other, it is based on regulation and control. But I'm surprised that you mentioned the exhibition "Family of Man"

by Steichen in this context. Was it really democratizing con-27
sidering, for example, what many critics have said were the
heteronormative and racist implications of the exhibition?

FT: The generation of art critics from the 1980s have made the
case against "The Family of Man" very powerfully. They have
called it racist, sexist, and nationalistic, even neo-colonial.
But if you go back and study the actual responses to the
show in that period and look closely at the images, you'll
find something quite different. Abigail Solomon-Godeau
(2004), for instance, is a very famous art critic and she said
that there are no pictures of black people and white people
holding hands together. That is not actually true (see Turner
2012). She said that there were more denigrating depictions
of African-Americans than white folks. Again, not true. I went
through and counted them. Pictures of Africans are there;
they were taken by African photographers. "The Family of
Man" presents a much more egalitarian world than most
critics think today. Yes, it has the kind of family ethos that we
found to be a problem in the 1980s and 1990s, but in its own
time it was seen as very radical.

Let me give you an example. Near the center of the
exhibition, there was a now-famous image of a polygamous
African family in rural Africa living in a couple of huts. To
the critics of the 1980s, it looked like a denigrating image.
It primitivized Africans and it privileged heteronormativity,
they believed. Critical voices say: "Look, there are no queer
people in this show, there are just straight people, they're
having families." Okay. If you go back and read the response
to the show, people who saw the show were amazed. For
them, the polygamous family image actually opened up the
possibility of different ways to organize sexuality, ways of
being different than they were. Steichen asked his audiences
to identify with polygamists. He asked white Americans to
identify with Africans and African-Americans. This is 1955,

just before the civil rights movement starts. It is the peak of the Cold War and a deeply racist time in America.

Another example: in the center of the show, there were four very large images, each maybe 10 feet tall. One of these images has Japanese people in traditional costumes, another has Italians, another has Russians, and another has impoverished white Americans. I cannot tell you how difficult it was, 10 years after World War II, for Americans to look at a large picture of traditionally dressed Japanese people over their heads and to be asked to identify with them. You know, my grandmother was still so angry about World War II and what the Japanese did that in 1988 when I bought a Toyota, she didn't talk to me for two weeks.

So, I think that if you go back and look at the material of the time, "The Family of Man" is actually a much more open show than the critics of the 1980s and 1990s have suggested. It looks closed to us now, but at the time it opened the doors to lots of different ways of being—prominently including anti-racist and antisexist modes.

ML: But it was this multi-perspective and multi-media environment that had this doubtful notion of democracy you speak about. This must be seen as a problem?

FT: I think that in the early 1930s, 1940s and 1950s, the multi-image environment, the multi-sound environment that I call the democratic surround, were forces for good. They were designed to produce democratic subjects and they were closely associated with a series of egalitarian political movements that we've forgotten. We've forgotten that in the wake of World War II there was a radical push for homosexual rights, very publicly. In 1941, a number of American intellectuals pushed very hard against American racism. They said look, if we're going to go to war against Germany and German racists, we have to fix our own race problems at home. We've forgotten those things. We remember the period between 1945 and 1955 as a period of increasing repression, of containment, psychological, political, racial, all of it. That's just not accurate. Or at the very least, it's not the whole story. It was a much more conflicted and open time. What actually happened—and it's even sadder—is that as the 1950s went on, the surround form lost its original political associations. After World War II, the form traveled to two places: it went to the art world and it went to propaganda exhibitions in Europe. These exhibitions were designed to promote American politics but also American commerce, and they appeared around the world. As they did, their original political ambitions melted away. The surround became an architecture not for a new politics, not for a new egalitarian social system, but for consumer choice. The anti-racist and the pro-sexual diversity critiques of the 1940s and early 1950s simply melted away.

You see this most dramatically in the 1959 American National Exhibition in Moscow. The exhibition was a showcase for the surround mode of display. The designers and architects Charles and Ray Eames offered a seven-screen multi-image slide show called "Glimpses of the USA," and "The Family of Man" was shown there, alongside huge displays of American consumer goods—everything from books and records to washing machines. Those who built the American National Exhibition hoped that audiences would conflate consumer choice with political choice and so conclude that democracy would improve their lives.

A similar process took place in the art world. The happenings of the late 1950s and early 1960s borrowed heavily from the aesthetics of the democratic surround. Yet they left the expressive politics of the 1940s off the stage. When I looked at archival pictures of happenings, I was completely surprised. I thought they would be radically open, radically diverse. On the contrary: with very few exceptions I saw young, white men dominating environments in which there were very few women at all. What women there were, were often naked underneath wet sheets or layers of whipped cream. They had clearly been made to be watched as objects of sexual desire. I can remember seeing no more than one or two people of color in a hundred images. The happenings were heteronormative, white, male environments. But they've been celebrated as environments of theatrical choice. Spectators got to choose what they paid attention to; they were surrounded by the imagery. What actually happened—it's so sad—is that the politics associated with the surround form in the mid-century, in the 1940s, disappeared across the 1950s. It became a kind of consumerist politics by the early 1960s, in propaganda exhibitions and art alike.

This had a real impact on psychedelic art in the 1960s. The art started to become deracinated, depoliticized. It became about personal experience. It became about consciousness. Young, almost exclusively white, almost exclusively middle-class Americans now began to offer up psychedelic media, LSD, and countercultural technologies as tools with which to achieve a new consciousness. But they did it in environments that were racially segregated. The communes of the 1960s were almost exclusively white; they were often dropped in the middle of areas where there were Mexican Americans or Native Americans who were ignored and pushed away. They ended up replicating the kind of contained American society that the 1960s ostensibly pushed against. So that's where the breakdown happened: in the 15 years after World War II ended.

ML: We have two similar problems for art as intervention. In the 1960s, a *depoliticization* of the artistic "democratic surround" took place, whereas in the 1940s/1950s we see a political and economic *instrumentalization* of artwork going for the "surround." Concerning the political instrumentalization, I also think of the exhibitions of the abstract expressionists in the USA and in Europe, funded by the Rockefeller Foundation, which was connected to the CIA (Saunders 2000). These were supposed to show the world: this is American art, this is against Hitler fascism and socialist realism. So, art figured as a kind of weapon in the Cold War.

FT: And that happened to the surround form as well. I found a document in the United States Information Agency archives and it shocked me. It was a declassified document from the early 1950s that explained how to use media abroad. We needed to act like psychotherapists, it argued. We needed to assess the psychological condition of the foreign people— were they democratic or not?—and we needed to stage a media intervention. Then, we needed to measure and see if our intervention was effective. Starting in 1956 during the International Trade Fair in Kabul, Afghanistan (Turner 2013b),[3] and for a decade thereafter, this is what we did: we built these multi-image environments in places where we thought people might not be democratic, and then we tested people as they left the building to see if they'd actually been changed. It started in Afghanistan (Turner 2013b)[4] and by the time it reached Moscow in the 1959 American National Exhibition, it was a very sophisticated process. We had notebooks; we had translators who kept track of

3   "The high-tech dome, the cutaway plastic farm animals, even the arrays of multi-sized photographs—all were built to channel Afghan desires for modernization in a Western direction. The environment was designed to offer visitors a range of choices as to where to place their attention, from a set of objects that had already been selected by invisible experts." (Turner 2013b)

4   "Collated by researchers and delivered to their American managers, Afghan responses to the exhibition could shape the design of future exhibitions, and perhaps even that of American policy toward Afghanistan and other nations…. In this way, visitors became elements in an extended feedback loop. By measuring audience responses to the exhibition, American officials could feed them back into the next round of exhibition design. Each iteration of the cycle would in turn, in theory at least, intensify the psychological impact of the next exhibition." (Turner 2013b)

Russian visitors' questions. We even had a computer there that recorded the questions that people asked as they moved through the exhibition. It's astonishing. This kind of surveillance I think foreshadowed our world. We live in a world in which we are invited to have experiences all the time, but we are very carefully monitored. You know, living in America these days can feel a little like living in a super-market with spies.

ML: So, we had artistic interventions by means of multi-media environments for a regime of capitalist-democratic beings in the 1940s and 1950s. This demonstrates that we have to consult the history of artistic interventions and their entanglement with politics and economy if we want to make interventions in digital cultures. Studying their genealogy should prevent the same mistakes from being made. Is there something in the concept and practices of multiple perspectives that we could keep as a democratizing method?

FT: I think we can keep the structure. The multi-image structure, I would argue, was extremely political in the 1940s and 1950s. It's powerfully political. "The Family of Man," you know, had about 800,000 visitors in the first months that it was open. It's been seen by millions of people over the years. Heck, its catalog has sold nine million copies, it's still up in Luxembourg, still on display. I'm not sure, but I don't think it has ever *not* been on display somewhere—since 1955. So that show had an impact.

I think the question to ask ourselves now is, with what institutions are we partnering, and what happens when we partner with those institutions? Also: what are we asking our viewers and our audiences to do or see? Are we confronting them with things that make them uncomfortable? Are we asking them to identify with things that matter? One of the legacies of the people I've studied that bothers me is that when they did "The Family of Man" and these other

image environments, they often asked viewers to have a
kind of one-to-one identification with a person in an image.
The individual was very much the center of the action there.
That is the nature of liberalism. But I would ask: what kind
of media can we make now that let us find a third place
between commercial or state institutions and sort of collaborative liberalism? Is there something in between in there?
And that I don't know, but that's what I'd be looking for. I
think the form itself is more flexible than we give it credit for
being. I think a lot of it is how we deploy it.

ML: Let's follow up with the kind of interventions artists did in
the 1960s. We see the movement "Art and Technology" as the
non-profit organization Experiments in Art and Technology
(E.A.T.) you mentioned in the beginning, or the hippie artist
group around Gerd Stern, the Company of Us (USCO) (Turner
2013a). They had been intermingled with Marshall McLuhan's
research in media (McLuhan 1964) as well as with industry
and technology, especially with systems engineering. And
they shared an interest in LSD (McLuhan 1969). Their aim
was to change people's consciousness and make them more
open to the world, integrating them into their technological
environment. What should we learn for today's interventions
from this environmentalization of perception and cognition,
this kind of becoming dazzled, going with drugs, opening
one's mind, and all this done by the artists, trying to offer
LSD-like experiences to their recipients with artistic means
in order to help them adapt to the new electronic world?
Do we come from an epistemology of multi-perspectives in
the 1940s and 1950s to one of being dazzled, drugged, and
opened in the 1960s?

FT: Openness is a word that was very meaningful in the 1950s and
1960s, but also very deceptive. When we think back about
McLuhan, when we think about acid and we think about
the 1960s, we're looking at a time when people became
what Buckminster Fuller called "comprehensive designers."

What Fuller said we needed to do was to take the industrial resources around us, pull them out of their industrial context, and use them to transform our minds and thereby our societies. LSD was one of those industrial resources.

The second thing that we have to see is that artists, like many American citizens in that period, were utterly fascinated by technology. So, when they took LSD they were doing two things: one, they were in some sense opening themselves to a new consciousness; and two, they were also just literally doing what the American military and industrial complex was already doing. By the late 1950s and early 1960s, the military had built computer systems to scan the far side of the globe, to see as far as they could. The military understood the whole globe as a system that could be monitored. Well, you know, in 1966, after the three-day Trips Festival in Long-shoreman's Hall in San Francisco, Stewart Brand, a famous 1960s figure and founder of the Whole Earth Catalog, sat on top of a roof in San Francisco and wondered why he couldn't see over the curve of the world. He hoped that LSD might help him do it. You know, that kind of thing is very powerful. It's a sort of weird imitation of military-industrial power.

The third factor, which is again something we forget now, was that electronic media in the domestic space were incredibly new. Television was only about 20 years old in the late 1960s. It totally changed things. Everyone used to have a big radio in the living room. The whole family could sit around and listen, that was one thing. But when you got a little record player and you could take it into your room and dance alone, that was a different thing. That was a big deal. And when you could get an automobile or a car and drive and be free that way, that was also a big deal.

So, I think one thing that McLuhan was doing was marrying the kind of system-oriented sensibility of elite military industrial thinkers to the new experience of consumer

technologies that many people were having. And a lot of
Americans, but especially hippies, who bought into Fuller's
idea of comprehensive design, tried to use those new
technologies as ways to gain the kind of insight, vision, pres-
tige, and legitimacy that the military industrial experts had
in that period. Now, this doesn't speak very well for many
artists at the time. And that's a problem. And I don't know
how to think about it. I admire a number of the artists from
the time a great deal, especially USCO, but at the same time
I can see them at least playing with fires that were lit in
the military. And playing with technologies that had other
purposes. It looks to me like they are playing at being the
kinds of people who are on the edge of destroying the world.

ML: The episteme of a resonant "Be-In" became crucial within
the artists' interventions of the 1960s. It meant that we are
an integral part of the technological environment. Where
did this Be-In come from, and do we inherit traces of it in
today's performative technological environments, with
miraculous and mysterious self-organized technical things
and infrastructures?

FT: I think all those things owe their origins to cybernetics. And
I know that Gerd Stern of USCO first learned of cybernetics
through a draft of Marshall McLuhan's book "Understanding
Media," which he got at a party from John Cage. So, I know
these folks were reading it. And you know the key cybernetic
insight, in Norbert Wiener's version of cybernetics at least,
is that the world is a constantly communicating system of
information. Things are just patterns of information that
happened to have acquired solidity, and you yourself are just
a pattern of information that has acquired solidity for some
period of time. The essential cybernetic insight is that the
entire world is communication. It's just literally information.
When we move our bodies in the world, Norbert Wiener
describes them as information systems seeking feedback.
We are like little machines. We bump into the chair, we bump

into the table and we learn that oh, this is the table and I'm me—I should go in another direction. In the 1960s, the idea that human beings were both communication systems in their own right and elements in a global system of information scaled right up. It became an almost mystical notion that everything was interconnected. Everything was one. As USCO used to put it, "We Are All One." It's a technology-enabled vision of being in constant intercommunication. And of course, that's also the vision behind the Internet, behind the World Wide Web and a lot of Silicon Valley today.

ML: If we are still in, the question may be: how to come out again?

FT: Yeah, how to come out is a great question. I think we have to be careful too, in a contemporary sense, not to think that the "Be-In" (being in) is the political statement that people in the 1960s thought it was. You know, in the 1960s there were really two countercultures. One was focused on doing politics to change politics, and we can call that the New Left. And the other was a sort of technology-enabled consciousness movement, mostly concentrated in a series of communes in the late 1960s. The Be-In is mostly in that second group. It's the tool or the technique that grows out of USCO's 1966 show at the Riverside Museum in New York (Turner 2006, Turner 2013a). Within the logic of the Be-In, we have only to put ourselves in the right environment. We can then understand ourselves as collaborative citizens, as parts of a system, and we can then begin to act in right ways. That's tremendously naïve. There's a desperate urge to just avoid politics completely. And when you avoid politics like that, you take up technology and consciousness, sure, but you also take up consumerism. You take things, you buy things, you eat things, you wear styles. And this is another place that the politics of the 1940s left us when they faded away. You just can't solve the problems besetting America by dropping acid and seeing patterns.

ML: Let's compare the Be-In of the 1960s with today's situation. In the 1960s, systems engineering was the important technology, which made an environmentalization of media, and the artists' Be-In could be seen as an answer to this shift to self-organized and self-referential techno-social systems. Today we see the transformation of systems into the infrastructure of ubiquitous computing, pervasiveness, and invisibility, in which everything is fine, like here in Silicon Valley. I would like to pursue the question of the heritage of the 1960s Be-In.

FT: We imagine ourselves as free in that world and we imagine our interactions with that system as completely individuated. When I pick up my iPhone, I think, "Oh, it's just me and my phone. I'll call somebody I like and I'll make a connection and that will be good." No! Apple's watching, other companies are watching. Even as I make a private phone call, my data are traveling who knows where. I am constantly engaging with institutions and I don't know who they are. That's not okay.

I think to understand what's going on now, we have to go back to the 1950s and 1960s and to the rise of a kind of managerial figure. This is a figure who appeared in industry and also in the arts. It was the person who designed the system and managed the system. When we talk about artists making systems art, what they were doing was things like the Pepsi Pavilion, done by E.A.T. for the World's Fair "Expo '70" in 1970 in Osaka (Turner 2014). They were designing environments in which people could experience their place in the system, just as the 1960s counterculture said they should, but also where the artist could be a computer-based manager of people's experiences. They were factory managers; they were bosses in a new kind of factory. And we happen to have a new kind of factory now. And the terms of that factory were set back there, in that mix of management discourse and artistic discourse. And that is something that we have to hold against artists of the period. I think we have to say, you know, at some level you collaborated in the development and legitimizing of a new mode of control, the mode of control we inhabit now.

Okay, so, that's the negative. The positive is, you know, Silicon Valley is not Berlin in 1939. There is a lot of power here, but it really is quite flexible. It's quite elitist, it's moderately racist, certainly sexist, in the technology world anyways, and these things are all true and they are all problems, and I don't see people building environmental technologies today of a kind that will help liberate us in the way that so many Americans tried to in the 1940s. But at the same time, I don't feel dominated directly in the way that I might have in a more fascist era. I do feel dominated though. And this is that thing, this is that mode of management that the surround form pioneers. I am free, but I am free in terms that are constantly being negotiated and set for me invisibly by managers, who work for states and companies. And my devices, my digital technologies, enlist me. They automatically make me a citizen in countries that I never voted to join.

ML: This managerial figure as a contradictory constellation of management, control and a free individual reminds me of the concept of a self that we might inherit from the 1960s. David Tudor invented, for example, an ambivalent concept of control and the loss of control as model for a self in the performance series "9 Evenings. Theatre and Engineering," organized by Billy Klüver and Robert Rauschenberg. In his piece "Bandoneon! (a combine)" he enabled a self-composition of the sound system, which he finally controlled by a switch device, interrupting all the sounds if he wanted to. Or Yvonne Rainer's piece at "9 Evenings": in "Carriage Discreteness" she instructed the performer via walkie-talkie to transport things on the stage in order to generate the impression of a freely self-organized system.

FT: Yeah! And that's a quintessentially Cold War American view.
What did the president of the United States want to do in
the late 1950s? He wanted to open up and set free the com-
munist peoples of Europe; the captive peoples of Europe. I
would argue that what David Tudor is doing in that sense is
something like what John Cage was doing in his music and
what Eisenhower was doing in politics. In the space of artistic
intervention, in the space focused on the subjectivity of the
listeners and the audience, the artists and engineers of "9
Evenings" are attempting to liberate sound in a way that is
entirely parallel to America trying to liberate the minds of
former European enemies in that same period. I think it's the
same cultural logic at play.

ML: There is another aspect of Yvonne Rainer's performance, and
that's paranoia. It was evoked because there seemed to be
some invisible control in the well-organized choreography.
Maybe paranoia becomes a form of governance, which is
perhaps important for us today because we know we are
being watched. We know it, but we are interacting nevertheless within our technological environments.

FT: So, in this context, it's worth revisiting Americans' Cold War
fears of hypnosis. Think about the movie *The Manchurian
Candidate*, done by John Frankenheimer in 1962. During the
Korean War, many Americans believed that the Koreans
would capture our soldiers, brainwash them and then send
them back to be weapons here. And now we hear about
ISIS and other groups sending their brainwashed citizens
here to attack us, and yeah, paranoia is one thing. But I'm
really struck by how "9 Evenings" and performances like it,
perhaps the Pepsi Pavilion too, seemed to offer spectators
the chance to imagine themselves as active participants in a
world of science and technology that was really much bigger
than they were. And in the 1970 World's Fair in Osaka, I'd say
three-quarters of the exhibitions were immersive environments. You see them over and over again offering a way to

40 be in control, experientially, of a world that's much too big to
control.

ML: I would like to come back to my question: how to get out of it?

FT: Well, in a lot of ways, Facebook is a structured world for permanent and perpetual happenings. Everyone participates.
You are surrounded by images. You pick your crowd, and
you get to hang there. It happens. I'm happy to report that
infrastructures like these are still incomplete. And that's
really important. I am pained when I go to a bar and there
are televisions all around me. I am pained when I go to a
café and everyone is typing on their computer or everyone
has their cell phone out. I am really pained when I see young
people who should be looking into each other's eyes looking
down into their cell phone screens instead. That's just heart-
breaking. So, okay. But you can still put it down, you can still
walk out into the world.

You asked me earlier how we might resist this encir-
clement. Artists and engineers often want to take up tools
and build something, either to stop what's going on or to
bring something new into the world. I think we need to do
something much more boring. I think we need to make
stronger political institutions. The state and its powers
of regulation are really important. You know, here in the
United States and Silicon Valley, I see the kinds of inequalities
that the tech world brings about. I see what Uber does to
its drivers; I'm thrilled that Germany is resisting that. I'm
thrilled to see the Germans, French and English bring their
regulatory regimes and their civic consciousness to bear and
push back on these companies. Because these companies
are rapacious and they will expand just as fast as they can.
I think that one of the best things you can do is slow them
down. Just slow them down and think about them. Watch
them for a while and think about them, see what happens. In
the States, and particularly in California and Silicon Valley, I

think we've lost the kind of collective civic sensibility that is
taken for granted in Germany. We just don't have that here.
We have a deep and rampant individualism. Yes, that might
be effective for innovation, but that's arguable. I would say
the Germans are just as innovative in their industries. It's not
good for imagining civic alternatives. For civic alternatives
you need a state, you need a civitas—something civic.

My question for artists who want to intervene would be:
How do you make a kind of art that draws us to a new civic
consciousness, that celebrates the institutions that promote
a sustained civic consciousness, and particularly that help
you work with people that are different from yourself? That
was the original ambition of the Committee of National
Morale in the 1940s. It was to build environments that let
you sympathize with, empathize with, and collaborate with
people of different races, sexual preferences, ideas, and
origins. Where are those environments now? I don't need
another technology to connect with my friends. I see my
friends anyways. Where are the worlds that will help me connect with the ones who are very different than me? Where
are the worlds that will sit me down with a refugee at a coffee
table and let me talk?

ML: What about art as intervention today? We see for example
so-called environmental art engaging in the development
of a consciousness for a relational being in the world as a
fight against the effects of the Anthropocene. Do you see any
traces of the history we discussed here in this movement?

FT: One of my fears with relational art or with practice-based
performance is that it still echoes so much of what was done
in the 1960s—after the politics that were attached to media
environments in the 1940s had faded away. There's a lot
of art right now where you enter an environment and you
participate in some way and that participation is meant to
be sort of political, but you're acting out some version of the

old happenings logic. That's not interesting and that doesn't help. I don't want to see agitprop. I don't want to see the kind of bad theater they had in the 1930s in the United States. But I do want to see art that sparks critical reflection. Not art that asks me to act out and even savor my own subjection to power structures that are bigger than me.

ML: Do you have any good examples for your preference?

FT: I think I would start with non-performative art, as a general rule. I think there is some beautiful photography right now. I think holding still is a good tactic. The power of the still-framed image is only growing in a time where images are moving all the time, circulating rapidly while we too are physically moving. In that context, something that demands we hold still and look is very powerful. There's a photographer named Wayne Lawrence, who published a beautiful book called *Orchard Beach: The Bronx Riviera* in 2013. Orchard Beach is an area in the Bronx, where very poor people go to the beach. And he just does beautiful, very formal portraits of these people in their bathing suits with their families. You have to see the people in them. You can't not see them. That's powerful—to see people who may not be like you. If you want to make the world a better place, that's what I would go for.

Another model of intervention would be a feminist model from the 1960s. I very much admire the visual artist Carolee Schneemann. And her performance "Meat Joy" in 1964 is a good example of taking the environmental sensibility that had been depoliticized and repoliticizing it. She rolled around on the ground with men and women, most nearly naked, in meat with blood all over themselves, at the peak of the Vietnam War. This was a time when feminism hadn't really been born yet—at least, second-wave American feminism. That's powerful. She gave you something to meditate on that was not a repetition or reclamation of the dominant style.

And I would compare that to some of the environments that we see today that are installed in museums. These new environments are highly technical. They surround us and ask us to integrate ourselves into technical social systems. These new installations are much more like invitations to psychotherapeutic adjustment and obedience than what Carolee Schneemann was doing. So, I guess, what I want to say is that performance itself is not necessarily a problem. But we need to find modes of performance that don't repeat the modes of power that we are already stuck inside.

References

Lawrence, Wayne. 2013. *Orchard Beach: The Bronx Riviera.* Munich: Prestel.

McLuhan, Marshall. 1964. *Understanding Media: The Extensions of Man.* New York: McGraw-Hill.

McLuhan, Marshall. 1969. "The Playboy Interview: Marshall McLuhan." *Playboy Magazine*, March.

Pias, Claus, ed. 2003. *Cybernetics: The Macy Conferences 1946–1953; The Complete Transactions.* Vol. 1. Zürich: Diaphanes.

Saunders, Frances Stonor. 2000. *Who Paid the Piper? CIA and the Cultural Cold War.* London: Granta Books.

Solomon-Godeau, Abigail. 2004. "The Family of Man: Refurbishing Humanism for a Postmodern Age." In *The Family of Man, 1955–2001: Humanism and Postmodernism; a Reappraisal of the Photo Exhibition by Edward Steichen*, edited by Jean Back and Viktoria Schmidt-Linsenhoff, 28–55. Marburg: Jonas Verlag.

Turner, Fred. 2006. *From Counterculture to Cyberculture: Stewart Brand, the Whole Earth Catalog.* Chicago: University of Chicago Press.

Turner, Fred. 2012. "The Family of Man and the Politics of Attention in Cold War America." *Public Culture* 24: 55–84. Accessed March 11, 2017. https://fredturner.stanford.edu/wp-content/uploads/Turner-Family-of-Man-PC-24.11.pdf.

Turner, Fred. 2013a. *The Democratic Surround: Multimedia & American Liberalism from World War II to the Psychedelic Sixties.* Chicago: University of Chicago Press.

Turner, Fred. 2013b. "Therapeutic Nationalism". *Cosmologics Magazine.* Accessed March 11, 2017. http://cosmologicsmagazine.com/fred-turner-therapeutic-nationalism/.

Turner, Fred. 2014. "The Corporation and the Counterculture: Revisiting the Pepsi Pavilion and the Politics of Cold War Multimedia." *The Velvet Light Trap* 73 (Spring): 66–78.

ARCANUM

CLAUSEWITZ

RESISTANCE

INTERNET

KAHN

BARAN

ENCRYPTION

2

Strategic Intervention and the Digital Capacity to Resist

Howard Caygill

What is the character of strategic intervention in contexts where there is a claim not only to a monopoly of the use of the means of violence but also a monopoly of secrecy? What options for resistance are available when the state extends its claim from the monopoly of violence to a monopoly of information? What is the quality and the conduct of resistance— its strategic options—when confronting not only the potential physical violence of state and corporate power but also its *arcanum*, the realm of secrecy and the exclusive control of access to information that it inhabits? Such questions immediately address the case of digital resistance, whether in the use of the

Internet as a means for coordinating resistance or in resistant interventions carried out on the terrain of the Internet. They assume specific urgency when it is understood that the Internet is increasingly assuming the character of an *arcanum*, or place where states and corporations pursue a monopoly of secrecy, which is to say, the goal of denying us our secrecy. What is a strategic intervention in a context where the state's claim to monopolize secrecy or access to information necessarily entails the surrender of any such claim on the part of civil society?

Arcana and the Internet

For some, the classic example of a strategic intervention in an *arcanum* is the Second World War. Once the *arcanum* of German and Japanese control and command—the Enigma coding of military communications—had been compromised by the work of Alan Turing and other cryptographers at Bletchley Park (Erskine and Smith 2011), what were the strategic options available for effective intervention? The obvious option was to use the information gained by the breach of military secrecy to secure short-term military advantage: if you know where the U-boats are you warn the ships in the convoys; if you know where enemy forces are and their intentions, you intervene in a pre-emptive response. But such intelligence-directed interventions would immediately alert the enemy that you had broken their codes— entered their *arcanum*—and they would respond by reconfiguring their codes. Another strategy consists of the selective and even disguised use of the information, intervening under the cover of fictions (spies sent and sacrificed, spies invented, bodies floating in the sea bearing false secrets), all designed to prevent the enemy from suspecting that their monopoly of secrecy had been compromised and their codes broken. In this case, strategic intervention becomes a play on appearances—giving any other explanation for operational knowledge than the real one. But this also entailed massive sacrifice—deliberately losing battles, only intervening when the secret of knowing the enemy's secrets is not risked. Neal Stephenson's novel *Cryptonomicon*—published in 1999 and widely read within the hacker community—fictionally elaborates on the scenario that the Second World War didn't happen but was a fiction, a cryptonomicon or fictional intervention in the *arcanum*. However extravagant the fiction, it remains the case that the field of operations research in the 1940s was close to the *arcanum* and many of its personnel—John von Neumann, Turing—would be crucial in the pre-history of the Internet.

Why Assange Missed the Point

In his 2012 dialogs *Freedom and the Future of the Internet,* Julian Assange referred to the "militarization of the Internet," or the "tank in your bedroom," "the soldier under the bed." For him "the Internet, which was supposed to be a civilian space, has become a militarized space … [and as] the communications at the inner core of our lives now move over to the Internet … our private lives have entered into a militarized zone." "We can't see the tanks," he concludes, "but they are there" (Assange et al. 2012, 33). This view contributes to his skepticism concerning the emancipatory potential of the Internet, his view that the possibilities for resistance that it offers are narrow and precarious. Referring to Egypt, but we could now add Turkey, Hong Kong and the United States itself, he warns that digital resistance is a high-risk gamble that once ventured, has to prevail "because if it doesn't win then that same infrastructure that allows a fast consensus to develop will be used to track down and marginalize all the people who were involved in seeding the consensus"—the "critical participants." But how to win in this *arcanum* where the odds are not in favor of resistance: What would it mean to intervene strategically? Assange's almost intuitive response is to expose and protect—to expose the *arcanum*, state, and corporate secrecy at the same time as protecting his own and his whistleblowers' secrecy by intense cryptography.

Assange's skepticism is a salutary warning to any attempt to mount a digital resistance, but it is important to reflect further on its central premise regarding the "militarization of the Internet" and its implications for an understanding of the limits and possibilities of resistance. My reflections will return obsessively to Carl von Clausewitz and his posthumously published *On War* of 1832 (von Clausewitz 1832–1834); Clausewitz is a central figure both for the development of the Internet and for assessing its potential for resistance. Is Assange right when he says that the Internet "was supposed to be a civilian space" but is becoming militarized? Is it not well known that it was always militarized and that its civilian uses were an accidental exception—space wrested from the military, or conceded by it…? It is, but without really appreciating the gravity and implications of such knowledge for the capacity to resist, prime among which is that if we move in a space that is a militarized *arcanum*, then our actions have to be guided by the appropriate rules and precautions: strategy.

Clausewitz's War of Resistance

Clausewitz is central to the elaboration of a modern theory of resistance. In spite of its title—*On War*—his posthumously published masterpiece is less about war—*Krieg*—than resistance, *Widerstand*, or more precisely the war of resistance. *On War* is not so much an analysis of war than an account of how to resist the emergent military strategy of the revolutionary nation state—France—through what the Peninsular War had called the "little war" or guerrilla, as opposed to the *grand guerre* conducted by the revolutionary armies. From the outset, Clausewitz offers a conceptual refinement that still in many ways eludes current strategic discussion around the theory of resistance; he is interested above all in the capacity or ability to risk resistance—*Widerstandsfähigkeit*—and not just its performative eruptions. Already on the first page of his first chapter, he defines the two objectives of war as: compromising to the point of destroying the enemy's capacity to resist while enhancing your own. As an idiosyncratic Kantian, his categorical imperative might be phrased, "act so that maxim of your actions enhances your own and compromises your enemy's capacity to resist." The rules for ensuring the survival and enhancement of this capacity are what constitute strategy for Clausewitz—it underlies his specific and historical discussion of the disposition of forces and of tactics. It is basically temporal in that it involves the survival or enhancement of the capacity over time—and in pursuit of the strategic aim of enhancement permits tactical retreat and evasive action. Furthermore, Clausewitz's account acknowledges the centrality of information (and misinformation) for preserving or enhancing the capacity to resist, and in particular the maintenance of secrecy. It was this view that earned him the admiration of Marx, Engels, Nietzsche, Lenin, Mao, Guevara and most recently perhaps his closest and most successful exponent, Nelson Mandela.

But Clausewitz was not only read by the left, his work was also central to nuclear strategy in the Cold War, on both sides, but especially in the emergence of strategic discussion during the 1950s in the United States. There were two opposed positions. On the one hand, nuclear deterrence originally formulated by the mathematician John von Neumann and pursued by President Eisenhower, and on the other, a neo-Clausewitzian position emphasizing survival and the enhancement of the capacity to resist. The latter position was associated with the RAND Corporation and its most prominent exponent was Hermann Kahn, who detailed its execution in an influential theoretical text *On Thermonuclear War* published in 1960. Kahn argued in internal RAND Corporation papers and publically in his book that the prime strategic objective should be less the avoidance of nuclear war than the enhancement of the possibility of survival and the continued existence of a capacity to resist or, in terms of operations theory, the means of ensuring continuous command and control. His underlying premise was that strategists should prepare the option of launching nuclear war with the security that the capacity to resist would survive a first or retaliatory strike.

Kahn's Resistance after Nuclear War and the Invention of the Internet

Kahn's bringing Clausewitz's *On War* into the nuclear age as *On Thermonuclear War* gives an invaluable glimpse into the quality and range of discussions in the RAND Corporation during the 1950s. He focused on the strategic options available under a "post-attack" scenario, advocating in the name of the RAND Corporation a series of pre-emptive measures to ensure the survival of the capacity to resist after a nuclear attack. He lays out a program of strategic planning dedicated to ensuring the survival of the United States but most importantly of its capacity to resist in a post-attack environment:

> Our study of non-military defence indicated that there are many circumstances in which feasible cultivation of military and non-military measures might make the difference between our facing casualties in the 2–20 million range rather than in a 50–100 million range (Kahn 1960a, 98).

The non-military measures include what will later be known as "civil defense"—fall-out shelters etc.—while the military measures focus obsessively on assuring the survival of the "command and control" structure vital to order, sanction, and execute a counter-attack. A pre-emptive strike on the part of the USSR is assumed to be directed against "command and control arrangements" in order to disable any possible counter-attack. Kahn predicts that "the bulk of their blow will be directed towards destroying, crippling or degrading the operation of our retaliatory forces"

(Kahn 1960a, 165–166) and in particular the system of command and control. He returns repeatedly to this vulnerability, which he describes as the "Achilles' heel" of current strategic doctrine, advising that "we should become more conscious of the central role that command and control is likely to play in the future as a possible Achilles' heel of otherwise invulnerable systems" (Kahn 1960a, 301–302). The latter vulnerability was regarded as critical for the survival of the capacity to resist under nuclear attack and received increasing attention not only from Kahn but also from other researchers within the RAND Corporation.

Kahn's strategic planning focused on putting into place reliable systems of command and control that were guaranteed to survive and continue functioning after a nuclear first strike. The planning entailed putting in place "some kind of information gathering network of data-processing centers that can receive and evaluate information, make decisions and transmit orders, all in a matter of minutes and even seconds. It seems feasible to build systems that will do this even when under enemy attack" (Kahn 1960a, 187–188). The substitution of "feasible" for "desirable" is characteristic of Kahn and the RAND Corporation's can-do ethos—if it was necessary to invent such a network, then it had to be "feasible." The only limitation Kahn seemed to place on the network was that it be analog, adding that "Nobody is yet willing to trust the decision of war or peace to a computer" (Kahn 1960a, 188). However, this was precisely part of the pragmatic response of a key technical researcher in the RAND Corporation to Kahn's strategic call for a system of command and control able to continue functioning after a nuclear first strike.

Kahn and the RAND Corporation's strategic requirements for ensuring the survival of the United States' capacity to resist contributed to the thinking that helped lead to the invention of the Internet. This is well-known, and a common response to the view of the military, Clausewitzian origins of the Internet is to present it as an interesting coincidence with few implications for future developments. However, such a genealogy is important for formulating strategic postures for resistance involving the Internet given that its origins were themselves part of a resistance strategy. The contributions of the RAND Corporation researcher Paul Baran are especially important in this respect. His work was dedicated to supplying the network capable of technically delivering Kahn's strategic demand for a survivable system of command and control. In a paper from 1960 prepared for the United States Air Force—*On a Distributed Command and Control System Configuration* (Baran 1960b)—Baran cites Kahn's 1960 RAND Corporation paper *The Nature and Feasibility of War and Deterrence* (Kahn 1960b) as motivation for his invention of a survivable command and control network.

Baran and Information War

Baran sought a control and command structure—or capacity to resist—that could survive a nuclear first strike. The option of bomb-proofing physical cables was explored but considered prohibitively expensive and unreliable. Baran focused instead on the idea of decentralized networks—first linking AM radio stations bearing only two messages—initiate and cease attack—then the telephone network, moving finally to theorize a distributed communication network with built-in redundancy and the ability to transmit discrete message packets. Baran later reflected:

> If the strategic weapons command and control systems could be more survivable, then the country's retaliatory capability could better allow it to withstand an attack and still function; a more stable position. But this was not a wholly feasible concept because long-distance communication networks at the time were extremely vulnerable and not able to survive attack. That was the issue. Here a most dangerous situation was created by a lack of a survivable communication system. That, in brief, was my interest in the challenge of building survivable networks. (Baran cited in Naughton 2000, 96)

In a series of RAND Corporation papers ranging from *Reliable Digital Communications Systems Using Unreliable Network Repeater Nodes* (Baran 1960a) in 1960 to *On Distributed Communications* (Baran 1964) in 1964, Baran proposed a distributed, decentralized network as the structure of communications most resistant to enemy attack. He also proposed that it be used to transmit bursts of digital information (later called "packets") that could arrive by any number of routes across the network to be re-assembled at the receiving station. This would ensure that the network would be neither fatally compromised nor overloaded in the event of an attack. Both the network structure and the digital modality served to enhance the system's capacity to resist.

While it is widely accepted that Baran's work indirectly provided the intellectual inspiration for the Internet, it is also held that its implications pointed beyond the military matrix in which it was conceived. It was an example of research of considerable civil import funded by the military but openly published and subject to scientific debate and public applications that far exceeded its contribution to defense (see Warnke 2011). However, as with everything published by the RAND Corporation, even the fact of publication was of strategic significance—and Baran's papers were no exception. The RAND Corporation was happy with the USSR knowing that the USA had theorized and was moving to implement a survivable control and command system. Indeed, the adversary's knowledge of the possibility and existence of such a system was essential to its working as effective deterrence. Even so, it might be argued, the implications of the research into distributed and thus decentralized networks eventually exceeded even this strategic context, providing the conditions for an emancipatory use or resistance of the non-hierarchical network.

Internet as Control

This view became a powerful ideological argument for an antihierarchical, even libertarian, view of the net that saw in its decentralized architecture an unanticipated possibility for non-hierarchical exchanges of information. Unfortunately, this view neglects other forms of control over the distribution of information that were also designed into the distributed network. We now know that debates within the RAND Corporation concerning distributed networks were accompanied by research into cryptography and the concealment of message paths and contents in a system with the potential to archive and make available to surveillance all of its communications. Baran's distributed network was also a cryptonomicon since a distributed network had an even greater need for cryptography, building secrecy and the control it afforded into its very architecture. This interest and the research it generated were secret and withheld from the published papers, which were consequently in no respect the unintended "free gift" from the military to a future non-hierarchical and democratic Internet.

The RAND Corporation's proposal foundered in the face of opposition from the telephone companies; however, Baran's papers were noted in the UK in the National Physical Laboratory (Donald Davies and packet-switched networks) and brought to the attention of another US strategic body—the Defence Advanced Research Projects Agency—known as ARPA (dropping the D). The detail of the history is complicated, but the same problem of a survivable network, decentralized but with compensating cryptography to ensure concealed control, persisted in the networks that evolved towards the Internet. In spite of their apparently non-hierarchical architecture, the history of these networks and their theoretical inspirations points to the construction of the Internet as an *arcanum* or space of secrecy.

This brief account of the concealed role secrecy played in
the early formulations of the Internet puts into question any
imprudent use of the Internet as part of a resistant strategy. It
would not be an exaggeration to regard the Internet as one of
the most prominent contemporary theaters for the struggle of
contemporary resistance movements to invent, maintain, and
enhance a radical capacity to resist. The struggle is conducted
on two main fronts: the first is resistance to the state's claim to a
monopoly of information and strategy and the second, resistance to state infiltration and surveillance of social networks and
the capacity to resist they have helped bring into existence. The
first front is the struggle for and against secrecy—the attempt
to sustain powerful encryption on the web against the will of
the state and also the effort to compromise state and corporate
encryption. This struggle has a history dating back to the 1990s,
in which Wikileaks, the Edward Snowden US National Security
Agency (NSA) exposures, and Anonymous are but the most recent
skirmishes. At stake is the state's claim to monopolize the information transmitted on the web and to archive its movements and
content at its openly illegal pleasure. Ironically, Chelsea (Bradley)
Manning and Snowden's whistleblowing was made possible by a
relaxation of the rules of access to the *arcanum* that was part of
the strategic response to 9/11 and the view that the USA's capacity
to resist had been compromised by excessive secrecy and the
reluctance of the intelligence agencies to share information. The
redistribution of the *arcana* of state secrecy, which was thought
strategically necessary to secure the capacity to resist a new kind
of enemy, paradoxically undermined it by extending access and
making its secrets vulnerable to public exposure.

The other side of the coin of exposing the *arcana* of state is
maintaining oppositional or civil secrecy through encryption. This
is a difficult and fallible project, but one which is pursued with
great strategic clarity and a keen sense of the paradox involved

in protecting civil society (Öffentlichkeit) through secrecy. This is an old problem, going back to the publication of Immanuel Kant's essay "Answering the Question: What is Enlightenment" (Kant 1784) in the pages of the journal of a secret society—the *Berlinische Monatsschrift*. The strategic stakes involved, however, should not be underestimated, since such efforts on the part of civil society constitute a challenge to the emergent claim to a monopoly of secrecy on the part of the state.

The ability to compromise the state's capacity to resist by weakening its monopoly of secrecy and hence its strategy is an important complement to the ability to use social media in constituting an oppositional capacity to resist on the part of civil society. The two campaigns are usually understood separately, but compromising the state's ability to survey civil society's use of the Internet is essential for the latter's ability to resist the state. For this is one of the simultaneous strengths and weaknesses of using social media to foster strategic discussion and to organize resistance. They can certainly deliver unprecedented levels of articulated and disciplined mass action, but also every step in constituting the capacity to resist and mounting resistance—as in the Istanbul Taksim Republic for example—can be traced and policed if the resistance is not successful. The very arts that permitted the creation of a capacity to resist on the eve of resistance can also undo it on the day after. Megadata can be used to trace associations (routine work for the NSA and other intelligence agencies) and to reconstitute with extreme precision the oppositional capacity to resist and its key members—militants and theoreticians—and even to proceed to their physical elimination (see Chamayou 2015). From one point of view, the web can liberate resistance and create a new capacity to resist, but from another it can also serve as the instrument for its decisive repression.

New Capacities to Resist

Rosa Luxemburg's dictum that resistant struggle itself gives rise to new capacities and constituencies of opposition was vindicated by the resistant actions in Hong Kong. Haunted by the memory of the failure of the Tiananmen Square occupation in 1989, which compromised the Chinese population's capacity to resist for over a quarter of a century, demonstrators associated with the two main strands of the Hong Kong resistance—Occupy Central with Peace and Love and the student Scholarism movement— adopted a strategy that they hoped would ensure the survival of the capacity to resist in the prospect of what Mao himself described in the 1930s as a "protracted war of resistance." Along- side the restraint and commitment to non-violence shown by the resistants—by now classical resistance tactics learned from Gan- dhi and the US civil rights movement—were a number of effective tactical innovations. The most striking was the conscious effort to limit the use of social media for strategic and tactical discus- sion in order to avoid leaving a record of the constitution of a capacity to resist that would help the authorities to unravel and compromise it at a later date. The demonstrators made wide use of the app *FireChat*, which makes an off-grid social network pos- sible using Bluetooth and Wi-Fi—ideal for mass gatherings. Over 100,000 copies of the app were downloaded in a day, putting the app to a use that doesn't seem to have been anticipated by its designers (they say on their website, perhaps with *faux naïveté*, "Whether you are on the beach or in the subway, at a big game or a trade show, camping in the wild, or even travelling abroad, simply fire up the app with a friend or two and find out who else is there"). The strategic benefit is nevertheless clear: one of the devices connected to FireChat can serve as a portal to the web and to exposed on-grid global social media; this device could employ deep encryption, and the decrypted messages then dis- seminated through FireChat in a way that left few traces for the state to follow later. This was an example of strategic prudence characteristic of both previous and contemporary resistant

58 politics; it complemented and further mobilized the resistant virtues of a non-negotiable passion for justice and courage. It testified not only to the need for resistance and protest, but also to prudence in the choice of means through which they are pursued, above all through what Clausewitz identified as the prime objective of a resistant politics—the creation and preservation not just of an act of resistance but more importantly of the capacity to resist.

Yet I should end with some comments on the desirability of a resistant intervention that frontally challenges the state's claimed monopolies of violence and secrecy. It brings with it a number of problems that might make us wary of adopting it too enthusiastically as a political philosophy or technique. First of all, the emphasis on strategy and enmity in the theory of resistance brings resistant politics too close to the model of warfare—perhaps politics and political reason are and should be distinct from strategy? In this case, the ever closer relationship between state monopolies of violence and secrecy might provoke disproportionately violent responses to any threat posed to its monopoly of secrecy and an escalation of conflict that can only compromise the capacity to resist. Furthermore, perhaps a resistant politics, however ingenious and imaginative its tactical innovations, is ultimately reactive, reacting against initiatives of its adversaries—as was the case in Hong Kong—and not initiating and guiding political change. Perhaps, too, resistance is too somber a politics, whose emphasis on the cardinal virtues of courage, prudence, and justice limits the emancipatory élan that is characteristic of revolutionary politics to questions of survival under conditions of repression and open attack. And finally, perhaps resistance is less a political philosophy than a politico-military technique, one that can be adopted in the name of emancipation but also in the name of reaction and repression. This leads to the final concern or question—if the *arcanum* is indeed an important site of current interventions and requires an appropriately encrypted resistant strategy, what implications will this have for the existence of a public sphere and even democracy?

References

Assange, Julien, Jacob Appelbaum, Andy Muller-Maguhn, and Jeremie Zimmermann. 2012. *Cypherpunks: Freedom and the Future of the Internet*. New York/London: OR Books.

Baran, Paul. 1960a. *Reliable Digital Communications Systems Using Unreliable Network Repeater Nodes*. Santa Monica, CA: RAND Corporation. Accessed April 9, 2017. https://www.rand.org/pubs/papers/P1995.html.

Baran, Paul. 1960b. *On a Distributed Command and Control System Configuration*. Santa Monica, CA: RAND Corporation. Accessed April 9, 2017. https://www.rand.org/pubs/research_memoranda/RM2632.html.

Baran, Paul. 1964. *On Distributed Communications: I. Introduction to Distributed Communications Networks*. Santa Monica, CA: RAND Corporation. Accessed April 9, 2017. https://www.rand.org/pubs/research_memoranda/RM3420.html.

Chamayou, Gregoire. 2015. *Drone Theory*. London: Penguin Books.

Erskine, Ralph, and Michael Smith, eds. 2011. *The Bletchley Park Code-Breakers*. London: Biteback Publishing.

Kahn, Herman. 1960a. *On Thermonuclear War*. Princeton: Princeton University Press.

Kahn, Herman. 1960b. The Nature and Feasibility of War and Deterrence. Santa Monica, CA: RAND Corporation. Accessed April 9, 2017. https://www.rand.org/pubs/papers/P1888.html.

Kant, Immanuel. 1784. "Beantwortung der Frage: Was ist Aufklärung?" *Berlinerische Monatsschrift* 12: 481–494.

Naughton, John. 2000. *A Brief History of the Future: The Origins of the Internet*. London: Phoenix.

Stephenson, Neal. 1999. *Cryptonomicon*. London: Arrow Books.

von Clausewitz, Carl. 1832–1834. *Vom Kriege: Hinterlassenes Werk des Generals Carl von Clausewitz*, vols. 1–3. Edited by Marie von Clausewitz. Berlin: Ferdinand Dümmler.

Warnke, Martin. 2011. *Theorien des Internet*. Hamburg: Junius Verlag.

NETWORKS

HACKING

CAPTURE

LABOR

DATA

REPRESENTATION

[3]

Intervening Infrastructures: Ad Hoc Networking and Liberated Computer Language

**An Interview with Alexander R. Galloway
by Martina Leeker**

Following a first wave of interventions that employed the style hackers have used since the 1960s—intervening in networks by mirroring their technology—a second wave is now engaged in questioning the needs and use of networks, claiming to re-think them through a perspective of withdrawal. One option for other kinds of networks may be "ad hoc networking," altering the structures, politics, and economics of commercial platforms as well as the pure functionality of algorithms. Instead of doing unpaid work, which we all do as users of the Internet, thoughtless about our data-behavior, a space of imagination and invention should be opened to enable creative possibilities.

62   Martina Leeker: In doing interventions in digital cultures we are confronted with infrastructures, like the Internet, which are ruled by algorithms. To intervene in such infrastructures, should we dispose of our knowledge of technology and its history so that we don't support the politics and regimes of data and control, but to come to forms of resistance? What relevance does your theory of the ambivalent existence of networked infrastructures between their statuses as closed, controllable and open, uncontrollable systems have? Is this ambivalence the basis of interventions in digital cultures?

Alexander R. Galloway: I am thinking of two styles of intervention, two waves even. The first wave is really about identifying tactics that are appropriate for technology and for networked technology, which is in itself very challenging because a lot of the old strategy and tactics from previous generations might not be useful or relevant. The second wave (or style) is more about transforming the network or technology in such a way that it's qualitatively different.

Let's consider the first one, with the hacker as a paradigmatic model. The hacker is the person who knows how to identify a flaw or exploit and take advantage of it. The hacker is someone who understands that networks feed on flow and exchange. They have a kind of contagious quality, making it easy to move things around and get from one place to another. The negative side of this, of course, is evident in phenomena like spam, email worms, and computer viruses. I consider this the "first mode" of intervention. It's a mode deeply rooted in intervention tactics inherited from the 1960s or earlier, where concerns focus on mobilization, collective action, and seizing territory. I'm thinking of rallying cries like "take back the streets" or "seize the media." At the same time, I'm deeply influenced by a group like Critical Art Ensemble and particularly their controversial if not inflammatory claim that "the streets are dead capital." In other words, people can go and protest in the streets, that's great, but it's a kind of Potemkin village because that's not 63 where power resides. Power isn't in the streets anymore, even as the police control the sidewalk with ever increasing violence. The traditional left was scandalized when Critical Art Ensemble made that claim, but I think there is something to it. Instead they suggest that we should consider alternative modes of intervention, particularly what they called "electronic civil disobedience." Today, we might call these rhizomatic or network-centric modes of intervention. That's one way to understand the first wave: exploiting the affordances of technologies. Some obvious conclusions emerge, not least being that blockading networks is useless. Distributed networks are typically designed to ignore bottlenecking problems. This presents a problem for classic intervention techniques that focus on blocking or seizing things (streets, territory, property, etc.).

The second wave or style of intervention is not so much a question of accelerating the qualities of networks or pushing technologies further—what we might call "hypertrophy," where the technology itself continues to define the field of action. Instead, the goal is not to let the technology define the mode of intervention. The first mode, the hacker mode, is like a perfectly formed mirror of technology. But the second mode asks: What if there is no mirror? Can we simply invent a new world that's off to the side? I see here a whole different set of tactics, particularly tactics like opacity and withdrawal. Some people interpret "withdrawal" as a kind of technophobia. Either that or as an indication of a latent romanticism—that we have to go and live in the forest and everything will be pure again. But that's not what appeals to me. I think there's a lot of interesting work to be done here around denying certain forms of digital capture. For example, encryption is endlessly fascinating. Even in something like the blockchain technology behind bitcoin— and let's be clear I'm very skeptical of a lot of the propaganda around bitcoin, but I do think that the blockchain is really interesting in the way that it uses authentication and encryption. Ultimately, I'm interested in trying to think about things that are *not* networks. Or things that are not reducible to the digital. We live in a kind of "generalized rhizomatics" today, so what might the alternatives be? Again, this doesn't mean we have to throw out technology, that we have to throw out our computers. It's just a point of inquiry: is there a way to think about technology that does not already assume the dominance of digitality and networks?

ML: Where are the problems in networked systems that we have to intervene in?

AG: The problems are all the classic problems of society: power, injustice, inequality. I'm primarily interested in technologies of capture. How do the individual actions of people get identified and marked or otherwise captured to be used for other purposes? It might be Google following your click trail, or Amazon following your buying habits. It's a huge topic, I admit. Within that topic, a number of issues are worth consideration. Personally, I'm interested in labor and see that today we're going through a new instance of the problem of unpaid labor. Capitalism has always relied on things it doesn't pay for. This can come in many forms: natural resources or the air, but also unpaid labor, whether it be unpaid domestic labor, or even in some cases slave labor (or prison labor), or forms of subaltern labor. Today, part of this comes under the heading of Web 2.0. Social media are very complicated and often hard to define. But at root we're dealing with a form of social interaction almost entirely captured and monetized in various ways. It's something worthy of intervention. Still, some people might be skeptical. Who cares? Who cares if Google tracks you, particularly since they provide a free email account in exchange? Perhaps this is a form of payment, a kind of "wage." I'm not sure. Still, what about all the people who don't use Gmail but are still

subject to capture? As a personal anecdote, my university
outsourced all of their email to Google, so I'm subject to
capture at the workplace and I don't have the ability to "opt
out" (unless I were to quit my job). In other words, numerous
people are still caught up by Google and produce value
that can be gleaned by them. If you make a blog, even if
you don't have a Gmail account, Google has access to what
you're producing and can feed into this system, extracting
value. It's a crucial point. It may sound hysterical to call
it a form of unpaid labor but I think it is. It may not be as
flagrant or violent as other forms of unpaid labor, as in for
example nineteenth-century industrial Europe, or other
forms of unpaid labor like slavery. But I do think social media
perpetuate forms of unpaid labor, and thus warrant our
concern.

ML: What can Google or Amazon take from my data and what are
they doing with them?

AG: Often I'll ask my students, "How does Google make money?"
Students usually answer that Google sells ads. In a mundane
sense, it's true, they do sell advertisements. But the
reason that they make money is not just because they sell
advertisements. They are selling advertisements because
they are producing some kind of value. How do they produce
value? Google is able to see the *shape* of the network. To
be sure, this shape is incredibly complicated. It's this kind
of fractal, tessellated landscape that's heterogeneous and
sophisticated and built out of masses of data. But, nevertheless, Google can see the shape of it—the topology, if
you will, of this massive database that is the Internet—and
through the various potential energies that exist in the
mountains and valleys of this hunk of information, they
can use such differentials to extract value. In his book *A
Hacker Manifesto* (2004), McKenzie Wark talks about vectors,
and I think that's a good way to conceive of these energy
potentials. Identifying high and low points, the vector defines

potential energy within data. It's translated very literally into what goes at the top of the Google search results and what goes further down. But the root question is value. To return to the earlier question, this landscape, this network topology, these millions and millions of micro-vectors are only computable because the networked self has a shape. And that shape is not created by Google, it is created by us. Google is a gleaner. But we're the producers.

ML: That's what I'm wondering about. We know about the regimes and power structures, but we don't stop producing data and supporting Google by doing so. Why?

AG: The web has always thrived on being able to identify the most utopian and aspirational things that human beings seem to want. Human beings like to communicate and of course they like getting things for free, downloading, etc. They like the kind of things that cell phones and computers allow them to do, to communicate with their friends and family and to build things. I am not questioning human aspiration. Still, my interest concerns what sorts of infrastructures, communities, and societies can we imagine that attend to human aspiration without perpetuating an elite technical class. Can we have non-commercial open source models? There's tons of examples of those that are still quite successful today. Not to glamorize the origins of the web, but non-commercial software and non-commercial infrastructures dominated the early years of the Internet. An important historical break comes with Web 2.0. Before social media, many of our daily tools were powered by open, non-commercial protocols. After Web 2.0, a lot of this migrated to commercial platforms. (Consider the difference between email or HTML, on the one hand, and a tweet or a Facebook status update on the other. The former are open protocols, the latter proprietary.) For instance, before Web 2.0 a lot of communication took place over email. After Web 2.0 a lot of the same kind of activities take place on social media platforms. It's an interesting historical transformation. Overall, we're witnessing a withering of the utility of open protocols and an increase in commercial platforms.

ML: What might non-commercial platforms look like?

AG: I've always been interested in movements that transfer attention and power downward, closer to people and further from infrastructures, institutions, states, and commercial power. *Ad hoc networking* has long fascinated me for this reason. And it's curious to me that ad hoc networking has never really succeeded, at least on a large scale. The idea behind ad hoc networking is that you don't need an Internet backbone at all. Communication jumps immediately from device to device in a local sense. Of course, programmers have built many different kinds of ad hoc networks, and even today there are ways to form such networks using Bluetooth, etc. Still, the adoption of ad hoc networking on a large scale would represent a dramatic shift. It would require compromises, of course. Expecting connectivity 24/7 is not going to be realistic under that model. High bandwidth might not even be realistic under that model. So, we might need to invent alternative forms of communication that make a tweet look long! What if the limitation was not 140 characters but, I don't know, a single character? What can you embed in one character? How many bits do you actually need? In other words, if ad hoc networking is going to work, it would have to be a network without a backbone, but it would also have to be a network without data. Or at least the data themselves would have to become smaller and smaller—which doesn't mean it has to be less useful or less interesting or less semantically rich. Those will be the kinds of interesting challenges faced by computer scientists and programmers. Perhaps we need smaller protocols, nano-protocols.

ML: But why doesn't that happen? What would be their political value and their level of intervention?

AG: It's not a technological problem. People know how to build it out. It's really a social and political problem based around power, particularly commercial power. Companies need the backbone. AT&T wants you to pay them 100 dollars a month for service. The companies that run the fiber-optic infrastructure have their cash flow and they need to keep it going. Not to perpetuate a conspiracy theory, but it's a crisis in imagination, meaning it's a social challenge rather than a technical one. The reason why I brought up ad hoc networking in the beginning is that there are quite mundane uses of it. If my friend is halfway across town and I want to send an email to her I could be using ad hoc networks to do just normal day-to-day things. At the same time, I could be using it at a protest, since these are the kinds of communication technologies needed in protest zones. In such protest zones, people often simply use the same technologies they use every day. They use Twitter, they use email, they're texting, they're using other kinds of social media apps. The difficulty is that a lot of these systems are piped through centralized nodes. Your phone calls and your texts go to the nearest phone tower. People talk about the revolutionary potential of Twitter, but it's still a centralized authority that mediates communication. How can it be a people's technology? Ad hoc networking would be tremendously useful in protests—and in fact it's already being used. The police can turn off the cell tower. Or they can use their so-called Stingray technology, a police device that mimics a cell phone tower. People's phones connect to the Stingray, but really their data are being collected. So, there's a lot of immediate reasons why one wouldn't want to have a device that has to go through a commercial or state intermediary.

ML: Then intervention should be thought of as a larger project, a larger concept of systems and education. It could be useful

to tell people, in workshops for example, how we could do it
differently.

AG: And to build these kinds of networks. Because they tend to
be very local and can be quite small. People are less interested in Facebook and Twitter these days. I think people are
interested in smaller systems. Of course, the Internet was
formed from man's desire for universality. It makes sense for
that period in history—perhaps the Internet was invented at
the last moment that anyone could still contemplate the uni-
versal. I'm not sure that's the point today. People seem to be
more interested in certain kinds of bounded conversations,
bounded forms of connectivity—not local per se but circum-
scribed. For instance, you might not necessarily want to be
on Facebook or Twitter with 20,000 people. What if you just
want to talk with 20 people. Several years ago we did it with
an email list, but now that's not the flavor.

ML: All the networked infrastructures are run by algorithms. You
said in "Are Some Things Unrepresentable?" (Galloway 2012)
that we can't make networks or algorithms visible in order to
understand them. How should we think of and realize interventions under these conditions?

AG: The first point to make is that data don't have any necessary
visual form. One might even go further and say that numbers
as such don't have a necessary visual form. Yes, you could
put two apples on this table and claim some necessary
"twoness" there. Still it's not entirely clear what data are,
and even less clear what they look like. I could show you a
hunk of data on a disc, and what would you see? What do
voltage differentials look like? It's just not entirely clear.
Therein lies the problem of data visualization and the basic
challenge of information aesthetics. Still, what's fascinating
is how similar data visualizations tend to be. If you were to
google the phrase "map of the Internet" you would come
up with endless representations of the Internet—and yet

they all look the same. There's a contradiction there. Information aesthetics exists, sure. But the picture of data is not pre-given. Of course, there are counter examples, but they prove the rule. Sometimes I describe this in terms of genre and claim that, today, genre is much more powerful than its putative opposite (modernism, the avant-garde, etc.). If genre indicates the dominance of a certain set of aesthetic expectations—the genre of science fiction, the genre of the western, the genre of the landscape or the portrait—we're living today through a "genre phase" for digital aesthetics, not a modern phase, or an avant-garde phase. It's almost like a new International Style, where the modern impulse evolves so far as to produce global uniformity.

The second point—and I sometimes get criticized for saying this but I think it's true—is that algorithms are incredibly uniform when it comes to the kinds of ideals and principles built into them. Algorithms tend to follow very specific structures. They tend to privilege a very limited number of virtues, virtues like expediency, efficiency, transparency, and clarity. There is a whole literature in computer science on what makes a good algorithm. What makes it well-functioning, what makes an algorithm beautiful or "elegant." Still, what about all of the things that have been eliminated from the conversation? What about an algorithm that isn't efficient? What about a stupid algorithm? What about a boring algorithm? What about a whimsical algorithm? What about an algorithm that is destructive? An algorithm that is pathological? A sad algorithm? Entire areas of human activity have been ignored in the development of computer programs and computer algorithms. Those are the ones that I'm really interested in. A number of people have started to explore this area. For instance, computer science has historically been dominated by men, and so some have attempted to write so-called feminist algorithms, even create feminist computer languages—with various levels of success,

and often eliciting vociferous antifeminist responses.
You can't imagine the level of anger that comes out of the
Internet when someone endeavors to create a feminist
algorithm. What would it mean to try to assign these kinds
of socio-political categories to something that is supposed
to be immune to that realm, given that it's "just" a technical
device—a false myth, to be sure. A few years ago, I started
writing something called the Liberated Computer Language,
an attempt to make a computer language that has nothing
to do with the tradition of algorithmic research and development. It can't be run on any existing computer—it's not
that kind of language—but these are the kinds of experiments I find the most interesting.

ML: But all modes of alternative networks would need a running
code. If I may compare it to the Netart in the 90s, intervening
in the Internet with noise and disruptions. These needed
well-done, running code. What would be the concept of interventions in alternative networks and codes?

AG: You are identifying a key problem. The underlying technology
relies on the concept of functionality—quite literally on
functions themselves. The function is a very low-level
technology in computer science. It comes by different names:
the method, the sub-routine, the function. Of course, the
function is also a central technology in mathematics, from
which computer science borrows a great deal. The challenge
is thus incredibly hard. It's like trying to write a novel without
using the alphabet. Often artists are forced into a double-
bind, either write code that works, or write code that crashes
the computer. There's almost no other option. And we all
know how easy it is to crash a computer. Computers crash
all the time. The most interesting artists are those who can
strangle the computer, not crash it. To strangle the computer

in a beautiful way. I'm thinking of artists like Jodi.[1] They are an excellent example of this sort of computer strangulation that produces beautiful outcomes. Of course, Jodi write code. They're totally technically literate and have a lot of skill. But they are using their skills to make the machine work in ways that it wasn't intended to work. In essence, we still don't know what machines are capable of, because so much of the effort over the years has been to try to produce machines that function correctly. Why don't we put our attention somewhere else? I'm sure we'll be able to discover endless amounts of interesting, creative possibilities. Instead of being monomaniacally focused on efficiency, function, expedience, outcomes, production—what if we pursue different virtues?

References

Galloway, Alexander R. 2012. "Are Some Things Unrepresentable?" In *The Interface Effect*, 78–100. Cambridge, UK: Polity Press. Accessed March 11, 2017. http://journals.sagepub.com/doi/pdf/10.1177/0263276411423038.

Wark, McKenzie. 2004. *A Hacker Manifesto*. Cambridge, MA: Harvard University Press.

1   Jodi, or jodi.org, is a collective of two Internet artists: Joan Heemskerk (Netherlands) and Dirk Paesmans (Belgium).

INFRASTRUCTURES

HABITS

HOMOPHILY

DIFFERENCE

QUEERING

PERFORMING

DISCOMFORT

4

Intervening in Habits and Homophily: Make a Difference!

An Interview with Wendy Hui Kyong Chun by Martina Leeker

In this interview, Wendy Hui Kyong Chun comments on different aspects of the constitution of digital cultures. Habits are viewed as infrastructures, and homophily (the principle that like breeds like), which currently grounds network analysis and fosters segregation, is called into question. Given these interventions, methods for engaging differences and queering homophily are highlighted in order to redefine comfort and discomfort.

Infrastructure as Habits

Martina Leeker: For our volume on interventions in digital cultures, I would like to speak with you about their technological and other conditions that we need to understand in order to intervene in them. Is there one critical point in digital cultures where it would be best to intervene? Where would it be best to start?

Wendy Hui Kyong Chun: I think you have to intervene at all levels: from hardware, protocols, software, and user interactions to how these are embedded in various economic and social systems and imaginaries. We need to constantly ask: Why are things the way they are? Since there is no one critical point, it is important to keep prodding at all levels. Also, we need to create broad coalitions because people have different forms of expertise: some work intimately with algorithms and machine learning and thus can help us rethink those algorithms (for example someone like Cathy O'Neil and her *Weapons of Math Destruction* (2016)); others focus on user interactions and social media. Again, what's crucial is that there are many different places to intervene and no one person can do everything.

ML: Absolutely, but we also have to realize that infrastructures are a big topic today, as technological fundament of digital cultures, constituted as networks, driven by algorithms. The question is: How do we intervene in them? To find an answer we need, of course, an analysis of their constitution, first of all.

WC: For me, the question of infrastructure is not simply technological—or human. For instance, my last book (Chun 2016) looked at habit as infrastructure. Habit, after all, is "second nature": it is something that is built rather than given at birth—it is not instinct. At the same time, it is nonconscious: it is in muscle memory and so "below"

consciousness. Like infrastructure, it lies beneath. Habit also
unfolds through constant repetition. Why is this important? Because sometimes work in the growing and important field of infrastructure studies tends to focus on technology, at the cost of human interaction, as though infrastructures were only technical.

ML: How do habits function? What is their most significant effect?

WC: Habits link us to the past, to old, seemingly obsolete technologies that live on in our interactions. Friends or the practice of "friending" has lived on past the demise of Friendster as a social networking site. Edsger Dijkstra, an early pioneer in structural programming, cautioned that machines and software foster certain habits of thinking, which fundamentally affect a programmer's mind. Habits mark openings in our bodies—we learn habits from others and in response to our environment. Most provocatively, habits are scars of others that live on in our repeated actions. Habit and infrastructures both support actions—and they also remain in intriguing ways. Habit provides a necessary counterpoint to rhetoric about disruption and new media as being viral. The fact that crises happen is not really that surprising. What is surprising and interesting is what remains after a disruption. The question is: What does a disruption make habitual?

ML: It seems that companies like Amazon try to make use of habits, for example, in the sense that they try to predict them via algorithms. So, another aspect comes up in this context, which is prediction. What do you think about the predictive potential of algorithms?

WC: They are fundamentally predictive; however, there is no way of absolutely verifying the results of these recommendation systems. Consider the Netflix prize, when Netflix offered a huge part of its database and a cash reward to any group that could improve its recommendation system by 10%. It awarded the prize, however, to the group that could best predict the past, that is, a part of its database that was initially hidden. This is because it is really hard to know what role any recommendation plays: How do you know a user wouldn't have bought a book regardless of the recommendation? How do you know a user wouldn't have bought any item that was recommended?

Homophily: Love of the Same in Networks

ML: I would like to bring in your work on homophily as a crucial model that has to be mentioned in the context of conceptualizing interventions. Could you explain the technological and conceptual sides of homophily?

WC: Well, you cannot disentangle the two. Homophily began as a sociological concept, which then became embedded within network algorithms as the easiest way to understand how connections form and remain. The term homophily came from two sociologists, Lazarsfeld and Merton (1954), who were trying to understand different friendship formations. In their 1954 article, "Friendship As Social Process: A Substantive and Methodological Analysis," they coined both the terms "homophily" and "heterophily" (inspired by friendship categorizations of the allegedly "savage Trobianders whose native idiom at least distinguishes friendships within one's in-group from friendships outside this social circle"). In it, they analyzed friendship patterns within two towns: "Craftown, a project of some seven hundred families in New Jersey, and Hilltown, a bi-racial, low-rent project of about eight hundred families in western Pennsylvania" (Lazarsfeld and Merton 1954, 18–88, 23, 21). Crucially, they did not assume homophily as a grounding principle, nor did they find homophily to be "naturally" present. Rather, documenting both homophily and heterophily, they asked: "What are the dynamic processes through which the similarity or opposition of values shape the formation, maintenance, and disruption of close friendships?" (Lazarsfeld and Merton 1954, 28). What is interesting is that—although this article is cited all the time—the breadth of its analysis, conclusions, and case studies are ignored. Network science now largely assumes that homophily, which is love of the same, is natural—that similarity automatically breeds connections. Thus, recommendation systems place you in segregated neighborhoods based on your intense likes and dislikes. As it's become a grounding principle, the world has become more and more homophilious. It does not just describe the world—it also now prescribes and shapes it.

ML: And then you go on to say that homophily is a way of creating segregation.

WC: Homophily *is* segregation. It assumes that love is love of the same, that you would naturally love to be around people like yourself, so therefore, segregation is natural. At the same time, homophily—because it emphasizes the actions of individual agents—erases the importance of institutions, economics, and legal structures (hence my emphasis on habit as infrastructure and the ways in which habits buttress/engage/are part of institutions, economics, etc.).

ML: What about heterosexuality? Can it be seen as homophily because it is a norm?

WC: Heterosexuality is actually a contradictory case: technically it's called "reverse homophily." Since many systems assume strong gender homophily, heterosexuality is an anomaly.

ML: How did you come up with the idea of working on homophily?

WC: Through an extensive literature search on networks, by reading textbooks.

ML: There are so many concepts of the "one and only correct theory" on digital cultures. Depending on the insights, they develop completely different concepts on interventions. How do you find the evidence of homophily? Homophily seems to be a point in which technology, the conceptual, and real politics come together.

WC: Most generally, I start with the fundamental concepts. I try to think as basically as possible in all disciplines and ask: Why is this concept important? What does it assume or mean? A lot of this work came from an earlier investigation into the predominance of networks across disciplines. I asked myself: What does a network mean across disciplines? What is a node or an edge?

ML: Could we still compare this approach to Friedrich Kittler's media-theoretical and media-epistemological tradition, the idea that we have to go back to technology in order to find the crucial points? Is homophily today's techno-culture?

WC: Homophily is basic on a different level. Homophily as a concept does not work at the level of electronics: if anything, heterophily drives electromagnetism. I'm also a little wary of Kittler's arguments based on his understanding of software.

Intervening in Homophily

ML: This concept of homophily, of loving the same, has been applied to network studies and their technology, configuring how networks and algorithms work?

WC: Clustered, how networks are clustered.

ML: Would it make sense for intervening in homophily to go to other logic concepts such as Gotthard Günther's trans-classical logic, or Heinz von Foerster's concepts of non-trivial machines?

WC: I think you need to change it on multiple levels. But I do think that reworking network algorithms and recommendation systems is really important, because we live in a world where the information we get is so selected—and it's selected

based not only on our history, but people considered to be   **81**
"like us." It's key that we rethink homophily both online and
offline. I think we need, again, to have many critical points of
intervention.

ML: In your texts, you mention the work of D. Fox Harrell[1] as an
example of intervening in homophily. Could you comment on
his approach to interventions?

WC: Actually, I view Fox as intervening into network science
more generally. Fox builds systems and creative artificial
intelligences (AIs). He creates different experiences that
force us to rethink social biases. At the same time, he
refuses to make race, gender, class, etc. simply static and
immutable categories. Part of his work confronts you with
discrimination and works from theories from Erving Goffman
(1956) regarding stigma.

ML: So, it's a way of implementing technologically but also on the
conceptual level, differences, in order to make us think with
differences, or to see things differently?

WC: Or to imagine dialog differently. His work comes from the
tradition of electronic literature. So, his question is: Can AI be
like great literature? Can it be like Ralph Ellison's *Invisible Man*
(1952)?[2] Can reading it change the world? Vi Hart and Nicky
Case's *Parable of the Polygons*—a really excellent reworking of
Schelling's segregation model—is also an excellent example.

1   For the work of D. Fox Harrell (2013), see: http://www.foxharrell.com/. "Fox
     Harrell is a researcher exploring the relationship between imaginative
     cognition and computation and his research involves developing new forms
     of computational narrative, gaming, social media, and related digital media
     based in computer science, cognitive science, and digital media arts. He
     aims to push the boundaries of how computers can be used for creative
     expression and social empowerment."
2   A novel about a black man rendered invisible by race struggle and its con-
     sequence: a precarious constitution of identity.

ML: What kind of interventions do you see for intervening in homophily by making differences? You speak about performance?

WC: Yes, I speak about performance partly in response to those who argue that because our actions are captured and are given more weight than our words, we can no longer give an account of ourselves. This may be true, but our actions aren't simply captured—they are shaped into what Phil Agre (1994) has called grammars of action. Capture systems, he argues, are based on a metaphor of human activity as a kind of language. So, they store, shape, and rearticulate our actions: they form them into grammars of how things should be done. The point is: even when we're simply doing things, we're still speaking. We thus need to rearticulate certain grammars and try to create different ones.

ML: Can we link this to Judith Butler's concept of the performativity of, for example, gender, or race (Butler 1990)? Her approach to intervening comes from Derrida's concept of iteration. It is about a kind of transforming of inscriptions by performing them. Could performing be like a silver bullet for diverse kinds of levels (technologically, by theater pieces, via artistic installations) in order to bring an ethic of difference into the world? Or, do we have to take into account problematic points of performance?

WC: At a base level, we can say that we are always performing. Even when we are being captured in seemingly spontaneous ways. Think, for instance, of how Donald Trump has become "authentic" and how he used reality TV to shape this authenticity. Reality TV, of course, is highly scripted and inauthentic: so, what is considered to be authentic now is completely scripted and performed. Thus, one argument is we're performing at all times. Judith Butler, amongst others,

of course, has argued that identities are always performative
and there is thus the possibility that things might go astray.
But there are also of course many other arguments within
performance studies, as well as Erving Goffman's work (1956)
on the social as itself a performance. There is a long tradition
of thinking through those terms.

ML: Would you recommend a movement of transdisciplinary
concerted action by people from different fields making
something like a net all over the world with rethinking and
re-performing? If so, how can scholars from the humanities,
or artists, work together with computer scientists and people
from network theory in order to change homophily?

WC: If network science looks the way it does, it is in part because
of the sociological theories it favors—that is, theories that
are relatively easier to model. It is already fundamentally
interdisciplinary. It is a question of getting different types
of theory into network science. But that clearly is not
enough—we need interventions at all levels. For example,
to combat abusive speech online, we need many different
forms of expertise: from those natural language processing folk to ethnic studies. For interdisciplinary work to
succeed, we need to start with a topic that everyone cares
about and realizes is very difficult to solve using one's own
methodology alone.

Queering and Discomfort

ML: In artistic interventions, we see "queering" as a method of
introducing difference and attacking homophily today. Thus,
looking at the history of queer studies and the hype about
queering, could there be a problem? If we are multiple and
should always be different, could these concepts unwillingly
support the politics and economy of, for example, gene
technology or neoliberal governmentality? Aren't critique
and intervention always eaten by the systems they live in?

84 WC: It is—there is no position that is not compromised and this is why queer theory is so important. Queer theory itself has also changed over the years. To just assume it is simply about drag is not correct—Sara Ahmed's[3] (2010) more recent work, for instance, about discomfort is really interesting, as well as Kara Keeling's work on queer OS (operating systems) (2014). Queer is best understood as a verb, a certain mode of operation. It can never simply be one thing. It also cannot be the solution to everything. There needs to be different ways of engaging things. Perhaps one way to queer homophily is to actually make it heterosexual.

ML: This means also going against the normalization of, for example, the heterosexual concept of family in homosexual relationships?

WC: I think the fact that heterosexuality both challenges homophily and reveals that homophily is hardly queer. Homosexuality and queerness aren't the same thing. But to be clear, homophily as love of the same does not even come close to doing justice to homosexuality.

ML: It seems that we have to be very precise and very differentiated in thinking about differences and queering. Perhaps some training in permanent discomfort could be a promising way?

WC: Homophily is constantly discussed as being comfortable, but it is hardly comfortable. If you're around people who are always like yourself, it is horrible. Think of something like segregated groups—these are filled with angry people. So, part of dealing with this is to refuse this offer of a comfort that is no comfort and to realize that what is allegedly comfortable is anything but comfortable.

3   See also Sara Ahmed's Blog "feministkilljoys," available at https://feministkilljoys.com/.

References

Agre, Philip E. 1994. "Surveillance and Capture: Two Models of Privacy." *The Information Society* 10: 101–127. Accessed March 18, 2017. http://pages.uoregon.edu/koopman/courses_readings/colt607/Agre_Surveillance.pdf.

Ahmed, Sara. 2010. *The Promise of Happiness*. Durham, NC/London: Duke University Press.

Butler, Judith. 1990. *Gender Trouble: Feminism and the Subversion of Identity*. New York: Routledge.

Chun, Wendy Hui Kyong. 2016. *Updating to Remain the Same: Habitual New Media*. Cambridge, MA: MIT Press.

Ellison, Ralph W. 1952. *Invisible Man*. New York: Random House.

Goffman, Erving. 1956. *The Presentation of Self in Everyday Life*. New York: Anchor Books.

Harrell, D. Fox. 2013. *Phantasmal Media: An Approach to Imagination, Computation, and Expression*. Cambridge, MA: MIT Press.

Hart, Vi and Nicky Case. *Parable of the Polygons: A Playable Post on the Shape of Society*. Accessed July 4, 2017. http://ncase.me/polygons/.

Keeling, Kara. 2014. "Queer OS." *Cinema Journal* 53 (2): 152–157.

Lazarsfeld, Paul F. and Robert K. Merton. 1954. "Friendship as Social Process: A Substantive and Methodological Analysis." In *Freedom and Control in Modern Society*, edited by Morroe Berger, Theodore Abel and Charles H. Page, 18–66. Toronto: D. Van Nostrand Company, Inc.

O'Neil, Cathy. 2016. *Weapons of Math Destruction: How Big Data Increases Inequality and Threatens Democracy*. New York: Crown Publishers.

OCCUPY

PROTESTS

SOUND

NANCY

BEING-WITH

HUMAN MICROPHONE

PEOPLE OF COLOR

5

P/occupy Milieus: The Human Microphone and the Space between Protesters

Ulrike Bergermann

A political movement trying to find new modes of communication, representation, and decision-making cannot use well-known media, especially when "representation" is contested. Can one voice speak for many people? Is the parliamentary mode of speaking for others to be overcome? In 2011, the protesters of "Occupy Wall Street" looked for other medialities and tried new "soft technologies" like the so-called human microphone. This article connects its use to Jean-Luc Nancy's concept of "being-with" as part of an ontology of a non-hierarchical thinking, and asks for the possibility of adopting it—even where the "co-appearing" people have not been equally "co" (given their educational,

racialized, and gendered backgrounds) in the first place when they became part of the "media politics of being-with."

An *intervention* is something that *comes in between*. *Digital culture* is a term vaguely denoting a culture that makes use of digital tools—or perhaps a mode of the digital tools' functioning. In any case, the title *Interventions in Digital Cultures* evokes the idea of halting fluidity, of blocking a space through which something is moving. Is any contemporary political action conceivable without the use of digital media? Are the images of resistance versus fluidity, of a rage against an ongoing machine—like in the famous story of the *sabots*, the wooden clogs thrown into sewing machines by eighteenth century factory workers to stop them taking over jobs—pervasive in all "interventions in digital cultures" thinking? If we consider the digital in terms of ubiquity, miniaturization, and connectedness, we see ourselves immersed in it with ever fewer spaces for pauses in communication and control. If we turn to the operational mode of "the digital," we might consider differential models of zeros and ones, of "on and off," and here, the concept of an intervention would not make too much sense either, as a myriad differences may offer a myriad in-between spaces to enter, and so the idea of intervention becomes intervention *ad absurdum*. At the same time, there did occur at a certain moment an intervention, a blockade that lacked digital (or any electric amplified) media in communication, which allowed for a fluidity, a being-in-motion within a radical democratic tactic.

A "social technology" called "human microphone" regained political and theoretical popularity during Occupy Wall Street's (OWS) occupation of Manhattan's Zuccotti Park in the fall of 2011.[1]

1   See Graeber 2011, 2013; Geiges 2014; Bryne 2012; Blumenkranz et al. 2011; Schwartz 2011; Mörtenböck and Mooshammer 2012. For the following, see Bergermann 2016a, focusing on the category of "individual experience" by Marina Garcés. Thanks to Daniel Ladnar and Nanna Heidenreich for critical readings.

Cut off from electricity and in need of amplification for their voices to communicate, OWS protesters reactivated the 1970s tactic of the human microphone in their assemblies: a person indicated they had something to say by calling "Mic check!" and the multiple answer "Mic check!" would start the process. After a few words, the speaker would have to pause so that people standing close enough to hear could conjointly repeat what they had said. One voice amplified by many, a process that could be repeated for those standing further away. Response had to be slow and was managed through hand gestures and lists of speakers. The human microphone was seen as a tool of a "real democracy" in which everybody should have a voice, as opposed to only one voice being heard as a representative of the many. "Democracy, not representation" is the oft-quoted interpretational formula of OWS.[2] Ordinarily, protesters demand specific political actions, but in this movement there was a denial of such an all too ready set of meanings and a claim of starting to find out what the demands of all participants were.[3] It was thus characterized by the ways discussions were held, decisions were made, and new procedures were undertaken—instead of a reliance on chosen representatives to speak, there was a radical inclusion of the many.

While parts of Media Studies were fascinated by the model of the swarm, because it could picture social behavior as technoid,

---

2   See the discussion by Isabell Lorey 2012. She unfolds the European model of democracy as grounded on principles of the representation of the people, designates these representational principles as an enclosure of a "power of the many" and of the fear of the masses (Lorey, 16–20, 27f.), and explains the occupations as a symptom of a "desire of the many" for a non-representational democracy in search of its form.

3   Another one would be the slogan "We are the 99%," as Jens Kastner argued: you cannot assume a unity of the 99%, neither theoretically nor empirically, but a unity should be considered as one always "under construction," in constant *becoming*. Nonetheless, it is the majority that suffers from the financial crisis, so one might think of a metaphorical 99% (a metaphor for "almost everybody"). The majority, however, does not share *one* point of view, not a *single* voice (Kastner 2012, 67).

and count the traditional humanistic ideas of responsibility and self-reflection out of it, the human microphone does address the question of the source of a message. First, in sending: speakers with prominent names were not especially welcomed (and the fact that three or four can be found on YouTube is a reminder of the fact that the usual suspects cannot be found). Secondly, in self-reflection: the regulated, quasi-automatic repetition of a message challenges its critical revision. This soft technology of an intervention thrills scholars who love fuzzy problems, not clean solutions. A lot about OWS's mic can be found in sociological and political writings (see Gould-Wartofsky 2015; Geiges 2014; Graeber 2011); philosophers in various genres discussed the human mic in terms of "the singular and the many" (see Nancy [1995] 2000; Kastner et al. 2012; Marchart 2013), artistic research analyzed its sound practices (Woodruff 2014;[4] Kretzschmar 2014), and it might be related further to cultural histories and discursive figures like the chorus, interpellation, or call and response.[5] Sound technologies and their respective philosophies have been invoked. While amplification organizes participation and silencing, the new assemblies of the 2010s rely heavily on the voice in that the spoken word is part of a multi-media network of computers, smartphones, and social media, and in that the idea of "direct democracy" calls for presence and orality.

The practical use of the human microphone recalls the old concept of the figure of hearing-oneself-speak, or rather: hearing-oneself-and-the-other-speak. A set of accompanying hand gestures is supposed to indicate whether the listener/speaker agrees or objects, even while repeating what was said, so that speech never has to be disrupted. The question of how possible objections can be seen by all, how they might affect the flow of speech, etc. is left open. Kretzschmar even welcomes

---

4   Thanks to artist Anna Bromley for this information; see also her work "Occupy Karaoke," available at: http://www.annabromley.com/occupy-karaoke-2013.html.

5   With a focus on the questions of sound see Bergermann 2016b.

the "amplification of affect" (2014, 155) through the human mic.[6]
"Authenticity," in any case, remains coupled with the voice (even
though the "pathos of presence" goes hand in hand with an over-
load of documentary practices, pictures, protocols, video clips,
etc.). Even the gross simplification of messages transmitted by
the human mic does not worry its advocates, who argue that it
was in the pauses between repetitions that people would think
and formulate precise wording, that the need for short messages
would lead to a concentration and compression of content, and
that the slowing down of communication, the conscious decel-
eration, would postpone the moment of political positioning, in
a step back from points of view that seem all too readily available (Kim 2011). The linking, even short-circuiting, of traditional
polarities—understood as a new political aesthetics—belongs,
I would argue, to the human/technologies/imaginary network
called human mic.

Dissonance/Unison

Black feminist activist and theorist Angela Davis, in her use of the
human mic, criticized its unifying mode of speaking and proposed
producing "dissonance, not unity, a noise in the system."[7] Nevertheless, more often than not, the opposite has been praised.
Mattathias Schwartz, the *New Yorker's* conservative commentator,
conceded that the point of OWS was its form and the slogan "We
are our demands" (2011, n.p.): the medium was the message;
form followed function. Some writers embraced a "suspension

6   The crowd would be "bodily taken over by the spirit of the speech" and
     would "throw back this enchantment immediately" (Kretzschmar 2014,
     157). In political theory, the importance of the *liveness* of speaking has been
     underlined since the French Revolution, as orality has been seen as an
     antidote to the corruption of the Ancien Régime; Mladen Dolar, on the other
     hand, has criticized the "political fiction" that democracy was a question of
     immediacy and as such a question of the voice (Dolar 2006).
7   Angela Davis at Zuccotti Park, October 30, 2011: "How Can We Be Together/ In
     a Unity/ That Is Not/ Simplistic/ And Oppressive..." (Woodruff 2014, 145). See
     Žižek's (2013) speech at Zuccotti Park: "Don't Fall in Love with Yourselves."

    of difference," as if Derrida's well-known critique of phonocentrism had been overcome: extend a repetition of something spoken to many people, they argued, and regardless of the space in-between them a sort of hearing-oneself-speak, or hearing-oneself-and-the-other-speak would occur, collectively.[8] However, Derrida's reading of Husserl had brought up a differentiation between the outer and the inner perception of one's own speech act, which allows for the perception of spoken words as self-produced and thus to perceive the voice of the other as your own (Linz 2006, 58; Derrida [1967] 2000); the break (*caesura*) was fundamental here (Linz 2006, 58). While a romantic desire to merge the one and the many may be part of the imaginary of the human microphone, there are other images and readings as well: multi-voicedness, the manifold (*Mannigfaltigkeit*), as Gerald Raunig notes, promotes a multiplicity of voices, an ongoing enfolding of the utterance[9] (2012, 123f). The single voices are not in *uni-son*, but resonate in different ways: in synchronization. This is not to say that the synchronized parts need one common pulse generator (like a hidden center). Kai van Eikels finds collective forms that have no representation as a whole (as group, party or even "movement," and even without the parts being aware of being a part [Raunig 2013, 12]) to be necessary and, what is more, finds the difference between the "parts" of these collectives to be

8   Woodruff asserts that the human mic often delivered "more lyrics than prose" (2014, 9). Kretzschmar states that the sense of the messages was often acoustically diverted into the bodies of the many "up to the suspension of the sense of the words" (2014, 157).

9   While van Eikels sees no need for a common script for the many, and Nancy sketches *com-munity* as the effect of a continuous passing, a Deleuzianian approach takes a different direction. Raunig proposes a "new schizo-competency" in making use of the "social-machinic relations out of which the enunciations of the multiple emerge" (2013, n. p.; see 2012, 124f). Whoever says "I" in speaking, listening or repeating speaks as a machinic subjectivity; this "I" does not aim at a perfect, unequivocal unison, but enunciates her own position, blurs author and audience, produces noises and multiple sounds as well, not in accordance but in consonance (2012, 125).

essential, too: without it, there would be no synchronization.[10] No intervals, it could be added, no intervention.

The (Mediated) Condition of Being-With

Another conception of "parts and the whole" also reads like a theory of assemblies and their manifestations. A retroactive reading of Jean-Luc Nancy's *ontology of being-with* addresses the one and the many of the assembly. His notion of being-with conceives of no temporal (or logical or any other kind of) priority of one over the other; there is no "we" prior to the subject, and no "I" before the community. Existence is always already coexistence, the singular does not come before the plural and vice versa: the world is "singularly plural and plurally singular" (Nancy [1995] 2000, xiv).

Nancy's attempt to rethink community without ideal subject or subjectivity, but through "being with," where neither *I* nor *we* are prior to the *other* and where existence is coexistence, does not aim at "being within a certain group" but at a set of mutual relations. "People... can only be grasped in the paradoxical simultaneity of togetherness (anonymous, confused, and indeed massive) and disseminated singularity." What is said in the context of a philosophy of being could be a test run for a very manifest form of togetherness, perhaps during the event of an occupation—in an attempt to paraphrase Nancy: the being is singular plural. You always start within the alterity of someone. Co-appearance does not mean to come out into a light, but being in the simultaneity of being-with, where there is no being as such (*an sich*) that is not instantaneously *with*. There is not

---

10   In talking about the politics of the streets, Judith Butler reminded us that "we can only be dispossessed because we are always already dispossessed." Greek philosopher Athena Athanasiou replied that it is not the same to "be" dispossessed, on the one hand, and "to become" or "be made" dispossessed, on the other. The language of philosophy here is just not *in sync* with the language of political life (see Athanasiou and Butler 2013, 5).

 a presence that is not a representation, spectacular, exposed, always co-existing. Being with/togetherness is a trait of being. Needless to say, no one would join a demonstration if there was nobody else, but there is more to think of in the midst of ontology and occupation here. People do not come in natural priorities and they *are* only insofar as they are already connected (Nancy dislikes the vocabulary of modern media, and he problematizes the inherent prioritizations of verbs and their propositions, so he uses the simple formula of *being-with*). If everything that *is* "passes between us, still," "between" is not the name of a space, it does not lead from one to the other, it is not connective tissue: *between* is the distance of the singular. "There is no *mi-lieu* [between place]." Difference has no representation, no place, no extension, and no thing was that was not with, *cum*,[11] as there is no natural state of being before the being was connected.

These well-known figures of deconstructive thought are transferred into an ontology, which can be indicated through the medium of language, maybe of writing (as in the hyphen between being-with), but overall, the price for this "horizontalism" is mediation: in theorizing the "with," there seems to be little to no concern for the "through": difference is not crucial. There is no *mi-lieu*, writes Nancy, nothing in between the one and the other, no instrument, no medium: "Everything passes between us" (Nancy [1995] 2000, 5).[12] The materiality of communication falls

11   What is proper to community, then, is given to us in the following way: it has no other resource to appropriate except the "with" that constitutes it, the *cum* of "community," its interiority without an interior, and maybe even its *interior intimo sui.* As a result, this *cum* is the *cum* of a co-appearance, wherein we do nothing but appear together with one another, co-appearing before no other authority *[l'instance]* than this "with" itself, the meaning of which seems to us to instantly dissolve into insignificance, into exteriority, into the inorganic, empirical, and randomly contingent *[aléatoire]* inconsistency of the pure and simple "with" (Nancy [1995] 2000, 63).

12   "This 'between,' as its name implies, has neither a consistency nor continuity of its own. It does not lead from one to the other; it constitutes no connective tissue, no cement, no bridge. Perhaps it is not even fair to speak of a 'connection' to its subject; it is neither connected nor unconnected; it falls

out of focus here, although even speech acts are based on such 95 a materiality. Seen from Nancy's perspective, the sound of the human mic would be eventful—it passes through bodies, space, resonances without any impediment whatsoever. The materiality and mediality of the bodies involved are playing different roles, though.

Temperature Checks and P/occupiers

Some were looking for the leaders, initiators and authors of OWS, some *Adbusters* tried to situate themselves as triggers and heroes of the movement (Geiges 2014, 79; Schwartz 2011; White 2017), and others may have been projecting ideas of self-emerging multitudes, but it was a participatory observer who, in fine detail, rewrote the histories of many small and greater movements, initiatives, and their technologies, writings and postings, that had to come together (Gould-Wartofsky 2015). And they could not have worked just as a sum of the old organizations and techniques. The search for new "social technologies" needed small inventions like the "temperature check." In order to manage what might happen in crowds between chaos and a fixed program, for example, to measure/feel when it might be a good point in time to start a discussion (people might be either too exhausted, too upset, too distracted, or eager to get a dis-cussion going at times), several "facilitators" would spread across the place and exchange their impressions of the mood in what in sum would be called a "temperature check" (Gould-Wartofsky 2015, 49). It was a kind of organizing of processes that was not upfront and could be removed quickly, with regard to possible

short of both; even better, it is that which is at the heart of a connection, the *interlacing* [*l'entrecroisement*] of strands whose extremities remain sep-arate even at the very center of the knot. The 'between' is the stretching out [*distension*] and distance opened by the singular as such, as its spacing of meaning…. there is no intermediate and mediating 'milieu'" (Nancy [1995] 2000, 5).

dynamics.[13] And there were sets of rules, too, regulating how to find out what to agree upon—rules that were always open to change, but could be referred to, nonetheless, like the "modified consensus" or the set of hand gestures [fig. 1, 2] (Gould-Wartofsky 2015, 8)—so it is not simply a super majority (as opposed to the 1% of the population that owns more than half of the country's wealth[14]) that the slogan "We are the 99%" invents, but new mechanisms for communication among people, one might say: new political technologies.

[Fig. 1] Occupy Hand Signals (Source: Wikipedia 2011).

13 It was criticized as well, for example by the anarchists of Occupy Oakland: facilitators would have been unable to "reconcile Occupy's horizontal process with its hierarchical inner life" (Gould-Wartofsky 2015, 105).

14 Joseph Stiglitz wrote in *Vanity Fair* ("Of the 1%, by the 1%, for the 1%," May 2011) that 1% of US citizens earned 25% of all the income and owned 38% of the nation's wealth; in 2016, "1% of the world's population will own more wealth than the other 99%" (Elliott and Pilkington 2015).

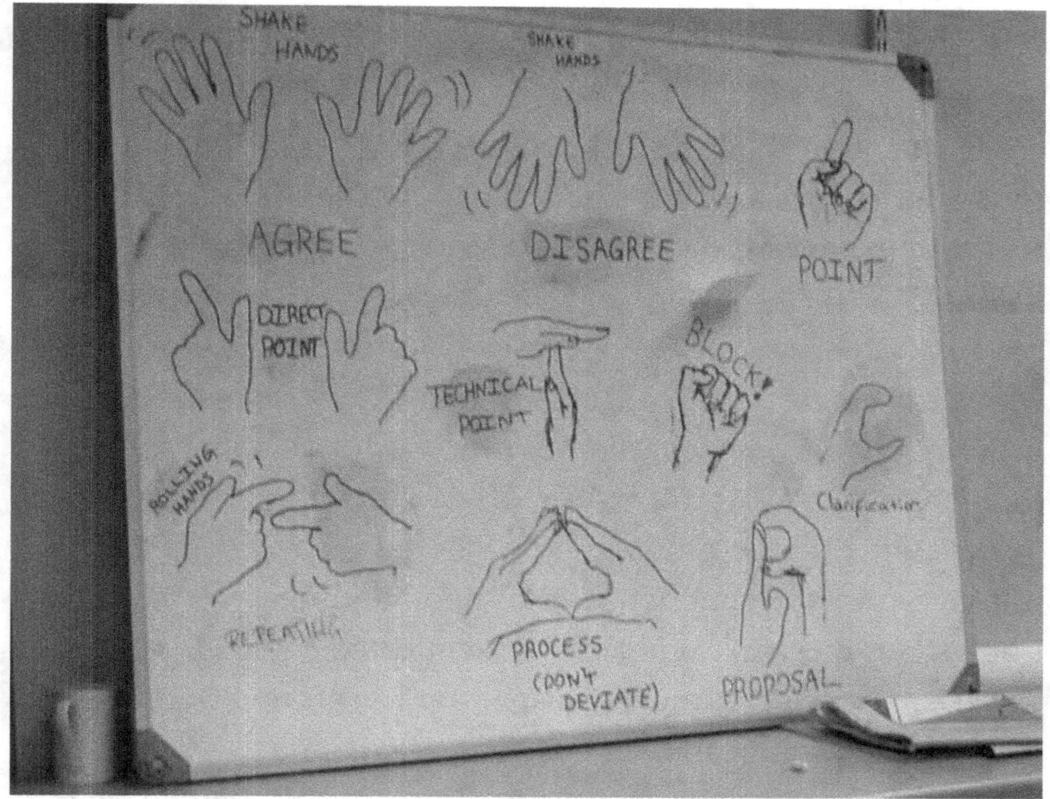

[Fig. 2] Occupy Hand Signals, Chart, London 2011 (Source: Wikipedia 2011).

Gould-Wartofsky often describes the sound of the meetings including the clicks of the camera shutters, that is: their mediated surroundings and their traces (Gould-Wartofsky 2015, 64 et passim) (while also warning of a "fetishization of process over strategies," 105). If the human mic was an invention, when did it emerge? It comes back to two astonishing sources: first, an unplanned "dress rehearsal" that occurred when (on October 17, 2011) some men and women stood on benches at Liberty Park and others standing below started repeating the messages, and second—or first—an older movement.

> Initially, the technique was an adaptation of a long-standing practice in American direct action movements, from civil rights to global justice, in which participants would chant, sing, or communicate information by way of call-and-response. The innovation lay in the everyday use of call-and-response, not only as a means of communication, but also

     as a mode of decision-making and community organizing (Gould-Wartofsky 2015, 67).

While inventions have histories, there is the need for opportunity, for chance and coincidence, to implement them. To come together, inventions need infrastructures, privately owned public spaces (POPS),[15] hardware and software, and many people who have patience, who remember histories and take responsibilities without claiming center stage. This "many" may, nonetheless, prove not to encompass "all." Not everybody had equal access to the human mic. As Gould-Wartofsky wrote after taking part in OWS and collecting mountains of footage, writings, and photographs, and conducting 40 in-depth interviews, race and class issues often excluded the non-educated and the non-white from resources and participation. The group POCupy demanded diversification of OWS and argued that "the 99%" were not coherent at all in economic terms, as an average white US household owned 20 times as much as the average black one (Gould-Wartofsky 2015, 98); Occupy Oakland quoted a Jamaican activist who criticized the occupiers for not speaking for those who needed it most; facilitators or organizers were mostly young white people with an education that made it easier for them to handle the new modes of communication. Michelle Crentsil, member of POCupy, reported, "We could walk through the park and yell 'Mic check!' And we're like, 'People of Color Working Group!' And all of a sudden it gets all muffled and nobody's repeating you anymore. I remember that one. That one really hurt" (98). Gould-Wartofksy continues: "Operational funds flowed freely to every group but the POC. Many who had come to the occupation to speak out found their voices silenced, their views sidelined by the facilitators and the drafters of key documents— often on the pretense that they had not gone through 'the right process' or spoken to 'the right people'…. Throughout the occupation, I often witnessed white speakers seize the People's

15   For an explanation of this special arrangement, see Reynolds 2011.

Mic from people of color" (99). After philosophical theorizations and/or partisan interpretations mainly given by white men who never asked themselves about their right or capacity to join the protesters, it takes a participatory observer, describing himself as an "educated white man in a blazer" (12), to reflect on his own point of view and participatory status, including his class/race/gender situatedness. Those who had better education were better able to make use of the elaborate tools of OWS.[16] The human mic, again, is not for all of humanity. The people's mic is not always the people of color's mic. During the protests following Trump's inauguration, Micah White, so-called co-creator of Occupy Wall Street, immediately tried to jump on another bandwagon and become the leader of an already existing anti-Trump movement[17]—and it was during the Women's March of January 2017 especially where it became obvious that black and

16   "Everybody should participate, but it tended to be the college-educated and the better off who had positions of influence, coordinators, facilitators etc., in an unspoken division of labor" (Gould-Wartofksy 2015, 218).

17   White's book *The End of Protest—A New Playbook for Revolution* (2016) is promoted on Amazon as written by the "co-creator of Occupy Wall Street." Suddenly, White sees the importance of women in OWS, or at least their strategic value: "It is significant that the initial spark that brought Occupy Wall Street into mainstream consciousness—the pepper-spraying incident on September 24, 2011—was an act of violence against women. The video of this event, two women screaming in pain surrounded by police, catapulted our movement into the spotlight. Looking back, I believe the gender of these protesters was crucial in garnering widespread support for Occupy. Joining the Occupy movement was also a way of fighting against patriarchal authority. Women played a fundamental role in every aspect of Occupy Wall Street, especially the facilitation committee that organized the consensus-based assemblies in Zuccotti, and women will make the next great social movement, too." Like in the magazine *Adbuster*, these politics are grounded in a deeply gender conservative (and antiqueer, antimedia) set of beliefs and its old-fashioned calls for a nature of men and women. "I can feel that women are on the brink of rising up against a male culture that has been fatally poisoned by pornography and video games." So, White calls for "a World Party that embodies our ancient uprising for people's democracy with a maternal twist" (White 2017).

  white protesters would not only be treated differently, but would also not always be aware of internal racism.[18]

P/occupy Milieus

If there are no mediations in Nancy's thinking of the *many*, and if his figure of the *singular* seems to always stand in the same position towards the many, which cannot hold true for different (gendered, racialized...) singulars, how, then, can we make use of Nancy's reflections on, and the practical mediated handling (his intricate writing) of, the problem of posteriority, which is always associated with superiority and part of causal logistics? Interventions do need *mi-lieus*, we see now, not simply because a *sabot* needs physical space to block machines or because the spatial metaphors transport ideas of re-sistance more easily. Interventions need *mi-lieus* insofar as re-thinking any space has to take into account how to connect in an unhierarchical manner, how this would be barred through supposedly antecedent structures,

18   "On Saturday, millions of women and men—organized largely by young women of color—staged the largest one-day demonstration in political history, a show of international solidarity that let the world know that women will be heading up the opposition to Donald Trump and the white patriarchal order he represents" (Traister 2017). Other writers included a critique of white protesters ignoring the racialized vote distribution (43% of white women voted for Clinton, 53% for Trump), different police behavior towards protesters, and the outcomes of Trump's victory (Elliott 2017); even the march's symbol, the pussy hats, were criticized because they "excluded trans women, as well as women of color. The pussy hats imply that you must have specific genitalia to identify as a woman. Additionally, they excluded women of color by insinuating that pussies must be pink. I guess this is why, for the most part, the only women you saw wearing the pink pussy hats were white" (Jones 2017). Nancy wrote about the "we": "We do not have to identify ourselves as 'we', as a 'we.' Rather, we have to disidentify ourselves *from* every sort of 'we' that would be the subject of its own representation, and we have to do this *insofar as* 'we' co-appear. Anterior to all thought— and, in fact, the very condition of thinking—the 'thought' of 'us' is not a representational thought (not an idea, or notion, or concept). It is, instead, a *praxis* and an *ethos:* the staging of co-appearance, the staging which is co-appearing" ([1995] 2000, 71).

and how to approach the task of de-learning to put oneself first in the line of perceiving and reasoning.

Philosophies of difference cannot do without taking into consideration asymmetrical architectures surrounding their differences. Interventions need *mi-lieus* to move beyond the two sides of a *lieu*.

References

Appel, Hannah Chadeayne. 2011. "The People's Microphone." In *Social Text Online*, October 13. Accessed February 6, 2017. http://socialtextjournal.org/dispatches_from_an_occupation_the_peoples_microphone/.

Athanasiou, Athena and Judith Butler. 2013. *Dispossession: The Performative in the Political*. Cambridge/Malden: Polity Press.

Bergermann, Ulrike. 2016a. "Un/easy Resonance: The Critical Plural." In *The Art of Being Many: Towards a Theory and Practice of Gathering*, edited by geheimagentur, Martin Schäfer and Vassilis Tsianos, 103–116. Bielefeld: transcript.

Bergermann, Ulrike. 2016b. "So-und: Zur Stimme im Human Microphone." In *sense-Ability: Mediale Praktiken des Sehens und Hörens*, edited by Beate Ochsner and Robert Stock, 207–233. Bielefeld: transcript.

Blumenkranz, Carla et al., eds. 2011. *Occupy! Die ersten Wochen in New York: Eine Dokumentation*. Berlin: Suhrkamp.

Bryne, Janet. 2012. *The Occupy Handbook*. New York/Boston/London: Black Bay Books.

de Haas, Ruben. 2011. "Occupy Movement Hand Signals." *Wikipedia*. Accessed March 28, 2017. https://en.wikipedia.org/wiki/Occupy_movement_hand_signals.

Derrida, Jacques. (1967) 2000. *Voice and Phenomenon*. Chicago: Chicago University Press.

Dolar, Malden. 2006. *A Voice and Nothing More*. Cambridge, MA: MIT Press.

Elliott, Larry and Ed Pilkington. 2015. "New Oxfam Report Says Half of Global Wealth Held by the 1%." *The Guardian*, January 19. Accessed September 3, 2015. https://www.theguardian.com/business/2015/jan/19/global-wealth-oxfam-inequality-davos-economic-summit-switzerland.

Elliott, Marianne. 2017. "Why the Women's March Made Me Think about Racism." *Medium*, January 22. Accessed February 6, 2017. https://medium.com/actionstation/why-the-womens-march-made-me-think-about-racism-3-b0eb1289d54.

Garces, Chris. 2013. "People's Mic and Democratic Charisma: Occupy Wall Street's Frontier Assemblies." *Focaal—Journal of Global and Historical Anthropology* 66: 88–102.

Garcés, Marina. 2006. "To Embody Critique: Some Theses. Some Examples." In *transversal*, June. Accessed September 27, 2015. http://eipcp.net/transversal/0806/garces/en.

102 Geiges, Lars. 2014. *Occupy in Deutschland: Die Protestbewegung und ihre Akteure.* Bielefeld: transcript.

Gould-Wartofsky, Michael A. 2015. *The Occupiers: The Making of the 99 Percent Movement.* Oxford/New York: Oxford University Press.

Graeber, David. 2011. "On Playing by the Rules: The Strange Success Of #OccupyWall-Street." In *nakedcapitalism*, November 19. Accessed April 14, 2015. http://www.nakedcapitalism.com/2011/10/david-graeber-on-playing-by-the-rules-%E2%80%93-the-strange-success-of-occupy-wall-street.html.

Graeber, David. 2013. *The Democracy Project: A History, a Crisis, a Movement.* New York: Spiegel & Grau.

Jones, Heather. 2017. "Despite Pussy Hats, these Intersectional Posters Shined Through at the Women's March." In *Wear Your Voice: Intersectional Feminist Media*, January 22. Accessed February 6, 2017. http://wearyourvoicemag.com/news/despite-pussy-hats-intersectionality-shined.

Kastner, Jens, Isabell Lorey, Gerald Raunig, and Tom Waibel, eds. 2012. *Occupy! Die aktuellen Kämpfe um die Besetzung des Politischen.* Wien: Turia + Kant.

Kastner, Jens. 2012. "Platzverweise: Die aktuellen sozialen Bewegungen zwischen Abseits und Zentrum." In *Occupy! Die aktuellen Kämpfe um die Besetzung des Politischen*, edited by Jens Kastner, Isabell Lorey, Gerald Raunig, and Tom Waibel, 50–86. Wien: Turia + Kant.

Kim, Richard. 2011. "We are all Human Microphones Now." In *The Nation*, October 3. Accessed February 6, 2017. http://www.thenation.com/article/we-are-all-human-microphones-now/.

Kretzschmar, Sylvie. 2014. "Verstärkung – Public Address Systems als Choreografien politischer Versammlungen." In *Versammlung und Teilhabe: Urbane Öffentlichkeiten und performative Künste*, edited by Regula Valérie Burri, Kerstin Evert, Sibylle Peters, Esther Pilkington, and Gesa Ziemer, 143–167. Bielefeld: transcript.

Linz, Erika. 2006. "Die Reflexivität der Stimme." In *Stimme: Annäherung an ein Phänomen*, edited by Doris Kolesch and Sybille Krämer, 50–64. Frankfurt a.M.: Suhrkamp.

Lorey, Isabell. 2012. "Demokratie statt Repräsentation: Zur konstituierenden Macht der Besetzungsbewegungen." In *Occupy! Die aktuellen Kämpfe um die Besetzung des Politischen*, edited by Jens Kastner, Isabell Lorey, Gerald Raunig, and Tom Waibel, 7–49. Wien: Turia + Kant.

Marchart, Oliver. 2013. *Die Prekarisierungsgesellschaft: Prekäre Proteste.* Bielefeld: transcript.

Mörtenböck, Peter and Helge Mooshammer. 2012. *Occupy: Räume des Protests.* Bielefeld: transcript.

Nancy, Jean-Luc. (1995) 2000. *Being Singular Plural.* Translated by Robert Richardson and Anne O'Byrne. Stanford: Stanford University Press.

Raunig, Gerald. 2012. "n-1: Die Mannigfaltigkeit machen. Ein philosophisches Manifest." In *Occupy! Die aktuellen Kämpfe um die Besetzung des Politischen*, edited by Jens Kastner, Isabell Lorey, Gerald Raunig, and Tom Waibel, 113–134. Wien: Turia + Kant.

Raunig, Gerald. 2013. "n-1: Making Multiplicity. A Philosophical Manifesto." In *transversal* 12, translated by Alain Kessi. Accessed September 29, 2015. http://eipcp.net/transversal/1011/raunig2/en.

Reynolds, Francis. 2011. "After Zuccotti Park: Seven Privately Owned Public Spaces to Occupy Next." In *The Nation*, October 14. Accessed February 6, 2017. http://www.thenation.com/article/164002/after-zuccotti-park-seven-privately-owned-public-spaces-occupy-next.

Schwartz, Mattathias. 2011. "PRE-OCCUPIED: The Origins and Future of Occupy Wall Street." In *The New Yorker*, November 28. Accessed September 3, 2015. http://www.newyorker.com/magazine/2011/11/28/pre-occupied.

Traister, Rebecca. 2017. "The Future of the Left is Female." In *New York Magazine*, January 23. Accessed February 6, 2017. https://www.thecut.com/2017/01/the-future-of-the-left-is-female.html.

van Eikels, Kai. 2013. *Die Kunst des Kollektiven: Performance zwischen Theater, Politik und Sozio-Ökonomie.* München: Fink.

White, Micah. 2017. "Let's have a World Party!" *Website of Micah White*, January 1. Accessed February 6, 2017. https://www.micahmwhite.com/worldparty.

White, Micah. 2016. *The End of Protest: A New Playbook of Revolution.* Torontc: Knopf Canada.

Woodruff, Jeremy. 2014. "A Musical Analysis of the People's Microphone: Voices and Echoes in Protest and Sound Art, and *Occupation 1* for String Quartet." PhD thesis, University of Pittsburgh, Department of Music.

Žižek, Slavoj. 2011. "Das gewaltsame Schweigen eines Neubeginns." In *Occupy! Die ersten Wochen in New York. Eine Dokumentation*, edited by Carla Blumenkranz, Keith Gessen, and Christopher Glazek, 68–77. Berlin: Suhrkamp.

Žižek, Slavoj. 2013. "Slavoj Žižek Speaks at Occupy Wall Street: Transcript." In *Impose Magazine*, September 17. Accessed September 3, 2015. http://www.imposemagazine.com/bytes/slavoj-zizek-at-occupy-wall-street-transcript.

Image Credits

[Fig. 1] Occupy Hand Signals. Source: https://en.wikipedia.org/wiki/File:Occupy-HandSignals.pdf

[Fig. 2] Occupy Hand Signals. Chart. London 2011. Souce: https://en.wikipedia.org/wiki/Occupy_movement_hand_signals#/media/File:Occupy_movement_hand-signals_diagram_bank_of_ideas_nov_2011.jpg

RESISTANCE

BIOPOLITICS

GLOBALIZATION

DIGITALITY

6

Digital Resistance in Digital Cultures

An Interview with Steve Kurtz by Martina Leeker

Steve Kurtz discusses a variety of forms of resistance to global capitalism, and examines their possibilities and shortcomings. Included are thoughts on occupation and street actions, digital interventions, and contestational biology.

Martina Leeker: Would you say that Critical Art Ensemble (CAE) is one of the "fathers" of interventions in digital cultures?

Steve Kurtz: CAE has been called that, and on one occasion, one of the "grandfathers" of interventionism in digital culture (and analog, too). I suppose there is some truth in this genealogy, but I don't know if that is the most productive way to look at it. CAE was just positioned well historically. We emerged at a time when three important shifts were occurring, and we were standing in the location where they all intersected. First, the political emphasis of the cultural avant-garde had all but collapsed. Metaphorically speaking, the new contract (that began forming in the late 60s and was mostly completed by the 70s) was that the financial classes would have complete control of this economy, and in return would allow complete free expression to artists to explore as they pleased—but political action was to be left out. Artists could make symphonies of noise, disrupt painterly convention, deconstruct theatrical narrative, or assault any other aesthetic convention of their choosing. By the early 90s, this contract was complete, and a clear split was evident in which those who refused to surrender their politics went in a new direction, ceased to care deeply about aesthetic convention, and focused instead on a cultural means of political disruption. This type of activity shared cultural DNA with the counterculture activist movement known as the Yippies (Youth International Party, formed in 1967),[1] the Haight-Ashbury-based guerrilla theater group the Diggers (1966), and the Situationists (1957)—and in a slightly more contemporary sense, the anonymous feminist collective the Guerrilla Girls (1985), the AIDS activist art collective Gran Fury (1988), and the AIDS activist video collective Testing the Limits (1987)—none of which were considered artists at the time by the cultural establishment. But there was a difference in the 1990s from what came previously, and that difference was due to the two other simultaneous shifts.

The second shift was the interdisciplinary turn. In the early 90s, students like myself who had reaped the benefits of the education struggles of the late 60s and early 70s were now coming into institutional positions. The borders between specializations were becoming increasingly fuzzy. Art as a specialization was no longer the only model for production, although it was still the dominant one. The borders could be

---

1   For all following groups or events the date of formation is mentioned.

pushed almost anywhere. At this time a new paradigm of art
making was born, but for it not to be destroyed by the elder
paradigm a third shift had to occur, and that was the mass
deployment of digital software and hardware on a consumer
level, as the graphical user interface (GUI), combined with
the launch of the World Wide Web. This gave the followers of
this new paradigm not only a medium to work with, but more
importantly, a way for the like-minded to find each other on
an international basis. With that ability, a critical mass could
be established that made possible a politicized movement
counter to the avant-garde. CAE was lucky enough to ride all
these waves.

ML: What are interventions to you and what are they for?

SK: An intervention is a minoritarian action (usually tactical) that
interrupts, redirects, or perhaps even transforms flows
within a given territory. For CAE, interventions are deployed
as a means to resist the many authoritarian tendencies of
global capitalism.

Art critic, cultural theorist and activist Brian Holmes offers
a very practical understanding of potential goals for cultural activists through a reading of Félix Guattari. The first
goal is to create existential territories. To create spaces
where a different type of affect is possible. Rather than
the fear and anxiety produced by capitalism, these spaces
lend themselves to joy, empathy, delirium, and solidarity.
The international Reclaim the Streets movement (begun in
London in 1991) is a good example. A second goal is reached
when a territory and the relations and behaviors within it are
reframed, reinterpreted, or problematized. A pedagogical or
consciousness-raising characteristic is a part of this type of
action. This type of work was common among those in the
feminist art movement in the US in the 1970s. A third possibility is the design, engineering, and deployment of tools
useful for resistance. Most of the time this is done by making

already existing tools do what they were not designed to do by re-engineering them to function in service of resistance—like Graham Harwood's social telephony operations (Harwood, Wright, and Yokokoji 2010). However, there are those who make their tools from the ground up. Tad Hirsch is an excellent example with his pre–Twitter protest organization tool, TXTmob (2004).[2] The recoding, subversion, or destabilization of signs and symbols is a fourth option. Most artists and designers seem to have a gift for this. CAE has worked in all of these areas in an attempt to reduce the intensity of the authoritarian tendencies of capital, and to establish an alternative biopolitics (Critical Art Ensemble 2002).

ML: Is intervening a ritual?

SK: I would argue that the heart of a ritual, whatever it may be, is to establish continuity, an immortality of sorts. We may be gone, but the ritual continues. In this manner, we link to past and future generations, thus establishing ourselves as part of the continuity of life and culture. However, rituals in this sense are also delusional. The maintenance of precise repetitions in evolving societies is not possible. Take the family Christmas ritual in cultures so inclined: a precise set of activities cannot be maintained. New people come into the system and others depart, changing the balance of needs and desires and the manner in which they are expressed. Fashions of all types change, so no matter how much sameness and family continuity is desired, the ritual continues to mutate as the years go by. Another possibility is to leave the rituals with professionalized classes (usually

2   TXTmob, an open-source precursor to Twitter, was developed by Tad Hirsch and the Institute for Applied Autonomy. The aim was to enable group cell phone text messaging among activists at the 2004 Democratic National Convention (DNC) in Boston and the Republican National Convention (RNC) in New York City. Thousands of people used it to share real-time information about protests and coordinate actions.

belonging to religious organizations). These institutions do provide more stability, but nonetheless eventually fail. Even the Latin mass has evolved. This is why conservatives and preservationists get so upset when a ritual changes in any way, no matter how perverse the ritual has become. The sense of continuity is lost. People can no longer take comfort in imagining that a person a thousand years ago was saying the same words and making the same gestures as a person performing the ritual today or a thousand years from now.

Interventionism does not care for continuity from the outset. That is precisely what it hopes to disrupt. So in a general sense, intervening is not a ritual. In a specific sense, we might tactically choose a ritual as a theatrical tool to produce an intervention, but it would be the end of the ritual within that context. We would have no need to perform it a second time. If the intervention were successful, there would be no need to repeat it, and if there were failure the ritual would have to be transformed into a new functionality or rejected as a mistake.

ML: What is the relation between interventions and transformations/re-organizations?

SK: Transformations are the best or worst outcomes of an intervention, or more likely, an aggregate of interventions. On a smaller scale, it can be a change in consciousness in terms of understanding or perception, or, on a larger scale, a change in policy, or a new form of social organization. Of course, interventions can go horribly wrong, as they are by necessity often grounded in speculation. Situations can turn from a threat of violence to actual violence, and control can transform into discipline.

ML: What is the difference between intervention, resistance, and critique?

110 SK: Resistance is the general category for any material or immaterial, active or passive manifestation that conflicts in some manner with the demands of the powers of domination. Interventions are a subcategory of resistance. Critique is a systematic analysis of an object or system that can be used to inform strategies or tactics of resistance.

ML: Do we need to think about or speculate on alternative forms of living, or about organizing society within interventions, or as interventions?

SK: Yes, as cultural activists, I believe that speculating on and experimenting with alternative forms of living are among the activities that we are called upon to do. If we could ever get this right, we would no longer need interventions. Organizing social formations as an intervention is among the experiments currently underway. The Occupy movement is an excellent example. Its very existence was an intervention in the social order, and became a public display of people trying to develop a new biopolitics—a new way of being together and sustaining one another in a peaceful, egalitarian manner. Occupy made a very compelling attempt to organize around the indefinite as a means to get to the emergent. The configuration had no leaders, demands, or goals—everything was left to an indefinite future. As this fuzzy network continued to exist, only that which emerged from this unscripted entanglement was accepted as meaningful (and perhaps only in that moment). Through the use of one of the oldest strategies of resistance, *occupation*, participants dumped the language of resistance of the past and let a potential "new" take form. Of course this action was incomprehensible to even the old authorities on resistance, and so there was no way it could be allowed to continue. Interesting questions in the wake of Occupy are: Should these experiments be done in public? And if done in secret, can the outcome be trusted?

And, of course, we need to keep transformational pressure on institutions that have an impact on how we live as well. While visiting here at DCRL, I was fortunate enough to work with Johannes Paul Raether.[3] He has taken up a narrative that seemed to have stopped progressing in the early 80s (to a large degree because of the AIDS crisis), and that is revolutionizing the family away from its cookie-cutter heteronormalized form. Throughout the 70s and into the 80s, radicals believed that the gay liberation movement could act as a vanguard toward a new way of conceptualizing and configuring the family (and for that matter, sexuality). When the AIDS crisis struck, and LGBTQIQ (Lesbian, Gay, Bisexual, Transgender, Queer, Intersex, and Questioning)[4] people were suffering on a daily basis because of the consequences of not being permitted to participate in family relations recognized by law, the political agenda changed. It moved toward marriage equality and assimilation. For the radicals this was not OK, but assimilation is what happened. Johannes is back struggling against assimilation and is asking for radical new forms, and is doing so through those formations suggested by reproductive technology, but with the difference that he horizontalizes the usual hierarchy of mothers. I find it quite inspiring that through the queering process Johannes has managed to turn a very dark technology into one of utopian possibility. The more of this work that is done, the better.

ML: What is the difference between CAE's *Molecular Invasion* (2002–04) [fig. 1, 2]—a biochemical targeting of a recombinant gene in order to destroy the plant—and plant conservation as in CAE's *New Alliances* (2011–12) [fig. 3, 4], planting an endangered flower that has legal protection under the law in

3   For his projects with queering avatars, see http://www.johannespaul-raether.net/.

4   An umbrella term used for anyone whose sexual identity, gender identity, and/or gender expression is not considered "standard."

[Fig. 1] Critical Art Ensemble and Claire Pentecost, *Molecular Invasion*, 2002–04. Installation view at the Hemicycle Gallery, Corcoran Gallery of Art, Washington, DC (Source: critical-art.net).

[Fig. 2] Critical Art Ensemble and Claire Pentecost, *Molecular Invasion*, 2002–04. Dying Roundup Ready plants (Source: critical-art.net).

[Fig. 3] Critical Art Ensemble in collaboration with Parco Arte Vivente and workshop participants, *New Alliances*, 2011–12. Transplanting the endangered species Cupid's Dart in a contested public space (Source: critical-art.net).

[Fig. 4] Critical Art Ensemble in collaboration with Parco Arte Vivente and workshop participants, *New Alliances*, 2011–12. Completed transplantation (Source: critical-art. net).

114   common urban spaces in order to prevent unwanted development in those spaces?

SK: For CAE, initiatives like these are all a part of developing contestational biology. We are trying to perform resistance through the frame of science and ecological studies as opposed to the frames given by cultural practices, humanities, and social sciences. The two projects that you are contrasting show the wide spectrum of possibilities of how science can be used. As we know, science is neither value-free nor politically neutral; we are calling attention to this position by making this fact very visible.

ML: CAE does a lot of work with biotechnology. Do you consider these projects to be digital interventions?

SK: Yes, on two levels. The simple and literal one is that key pieces of hardware and software are digital. Without such advancements, molecular biology would be at a near standstill. The more important level is that genetics, molecular biology, and synthetic biology developed along a parallel course with computer science and engineering. This parallel development is due to a shared set of analytic metaphors.

One fundamental scientific principle of the cosmos is that order comes from chaos, which comes from order. Digital engineering challenged the universality of this contention by showing that order comes from order (replication). Even science has had to contend with the advancement of the digital paradigm on a cosmological level. True, the elder sciences of physics and chemistry have held tenaciously to their analogic version of the cosmos, but the youthful discipline of biology, in a sublime moment of Oedipal revolution, has rejected the analogic model of its elders as being useless to its pursuits. Central to this discussion is the discovery of DNA. By the 1940s, it was already known that heredity is controlled by genes; that genes are located on chromosomes found in cell nuclei; and that genes are

produced by DNA. However, DNA was not really under-**115**
stood in terms of its full function and potential. It was not
until Crick and Watson were able to imagine the structure
of DNA that its true potential was realized. According to
human genome scientist Maynard Olson, Crick and Watson's
discovery was meaningful because it occurred within the
atmosphere of a formalized digital paradigm. They intuitively
understood that DNA was not analogic (order from chaos),
but instead digital (order from order). This type of mod-
eling made possible the biological understanding of the
production of life. Information replication in the body is
analogous to digital copying on a computer. Information is
stored as DNA (in a base-4 format, rather than in a base-2
format as used by computers), and replicates itself when
cells divide. Now that this piece of information is understood,
humans can intervene in the once autonomous molecular
systems of reproduction. This organic frontier now has
no borders because the basics of DNA become intelligible
when one analyzes them using the digital model of information storage, recognition, retrieval, and replication.
Digital humans, animals, food, and medicine are now in the
marketplace.

ML: How do you see the relationship between information and
communication technology (ICT) and biotechnology?

SK: ICT has been a revolution of scale. This technology has
exploded over the past three decades, and has made things
possible that were only vague possibilities to those in power
only a half century ago, including the total surveillance state,
posthuman financial exchanges (like high-speed trading),
and a true global economy. While international trade may
have existed for centuries, the national economies were
fairly separate. Now, a problem in one trading partner's
economy is a problem for all partners. The interdependence
is quite profound. Another way I could put it is that Paul
Virilio's global accident is now possible. In the West, the roots

of the globalization project go back to the Roman Empire, so in terms of globalization and its spectacle, it is really more of the same, only now on a heretofore unimaginable scale and with a digital paradigm. As we have discussed, I believe biotech to be a part of this same paradigm, but it is truly new and revolutionary. ICT has been enveloping us for many decades in the West, and its goal has primarily been to inscribe bodies with capitalist imperatives and to maintain order through mediation. CAE always thought that while we cannot escape the spectacle, our bodies, con-sciousness, and the organic inner world could maintain a semi-autonomous position. Now there is nowhere capital cannot reach. We are witnessing the beginning of a massive redesign of the organic order—to one that better suits the needs of capitalism—whether of its creatures (for functional or decorative purpose), or its plants and crops, or, to a growing extent, the human body. With new reproductive technologies, the potential for a new, voluntary form of eugenics becomes possible. This would not consist simply of selection for health or physical "normality," but of potential predispositions that would make a person more competitive and compliant in the marketplace. In this postnatural world, the exterior forces of the social and economic spheres can link to predispositions programmed into humans. Tempera-ment can be managed, and desire directed.

ML: Do you see digital models coming to dominate politics as well?

SK: That is a very difficult question to sort through at this point in history. My belief is that in the West, the tendency is toward the digital, especially in the US. I say this not because the US is so forward thinking, but because the way that its political system is designed transforms so much of pol-itics into marketing. Marketing and mass communications are dominated by the digital. Throw in click-politics, and it becomes hard to deny the power of the digital in the political sphere. However, turmoil over recent elections in the Western world may indicate that embodied politics may not be a total anachronism in digital cultures.

That said, we have to be careful not to stay in our digital bubble. We see the result of doing so from media theorists and tech developers quite frequently. They can forget that most of the world does not have relationships with Facebook, apps, surveillance, or ubiquitous computing, and that forgetfulness leads to ridiculous assertions like "The Egyptian revolution was a digital revolution." Such nonsense. Sure, there may have been some young people with digital skills who were using digital platforms to get their message out, but I do not believe that was representative of the overall event. I wasn't there, so I can't speak from experience, but we can look at the basic statistics. The poverty rate in Egypt is over 50% and extreme poverty is 28%. Then there is another substantial sector of the population (unfortunately, it is hard to find a reliable statistic) that is getting by day to day, but that is it. This is not a situation for robust sales and deployment of digital media. Not to mention that the literacy rate is extremely low (26% are completely illiterate). Digital communication is by no means the dominant form there. The narrative of the Egyptian revolution as a digital revolution is a publicity stunt that is a white-washing of corporations like Google, Facebook, and Twitter as progressive, and as delivering revolutionary products that change the world in a utopian manner. Yet we now know with certainty after the Manning and Snowden revelations how much the digital revolution has contributed to current global dystopian tendencies.

ML: Has the utopian moment passed for digital cultures and if yes, what does this mean for interventions in these cultures?

SK: Oh yes, if there ever was one to begin with. Perhaps the moment was there when the culture was limited to scientists exchanging data over the Internet, but as soon as it became a technical system assimilated into capitalist political economy, the party was over. For example, one of the most common promises that accompanies any new technology is that it will reduce labor time, with the implication that there will be more leisure time. Of course, the opposite happens, whether the new technology is a steam engine or a computer. Production rates are increased and labor is intensified. With digital technology and its propensity for miniaturization, workers were struck twice in that they were either given or had to buy their own (!) tools of labor (cell phone and laptop) that transformed them into permanent work platforms. Digital workers are always on call and ready to work. And if that weren't enough, these same tools evolved into the means for governments and businesses to keep individuals under surveillance at all times.

I know there are those individuals who claim surveillance is fine; privacy is dead—all well and good. If corporations are storing, analyzing, buying, and selling our metadata, it is only so they can better understand our needs and desires so they might serve us better. And if the government is storing and analyzing our metadata, it's only because they need it to keep the nation secure and orderly. Of course, these ideas are all nonsense. Governments are using this technology to expand their disciplinary apparatus to be used in a manner beyond that of neutralizing criminality, while corporations are looking for a way to construct in us a desire for their goods and services. Surveillance makes such goals possible, and the deeper they get into our lives, the more we become managed and controlled. And let's not forget what a profitable commodity information is.

The truly aggravating part of all this is that it didn't have to be this way. We could live in a metadata-free society. The knowledge about how to do it is there, but it won't be done because liberty like that is completely unacceptable to capitalism. Even the universities are complicit. Having spent 35 years of my life as an educator, I watched critical thinking be slowly exorcized from the university and replaced with neoliberal business strategies, and nowhere has that had a worse impact than in science, technology, engineering, and math (STEM). The culture of STEM is a problem-solving one. The unfortunate part of this method is that it is contained within a bubble of wealth, in conjunction with a very specialized point of view. In practice, this manifests as total focus on the problem and its solution, with no thought about the consequence of any solution once it is out in the world and subject to corporate and state policy. Most of the dystopic consequences of digital technology are tragedies in engineering. I realize that powerful outside forces are in play—but still, there are elements within STEM that technocrats do control, and therefore should do something about, like introducing more critical thinking, ethics, and sociological and historical analysis.

So yes, the utopian moment is gone. It can still exist for individuals, but a systemic change would require a reconstruction of the digital infrastructure, or at the very least a radical revision of software. Choices have been made (and not democratically), a lot of bad engineering has happened, and we are too far down the road to start over.

ML: What is CAE working on next?

SK: Necropolitics and ecological struggle, but that is a topic for another interview.

References

Critical Art Ensemble. 2002. *Molecular Invasion*. New York: Autonomedia. Accessed October 2, 2017. http://www.critical-art.net/books/molecular/.
Critical Art Ensemble. 2011–12. *New Alliances*. Accessed October 2, 2017. http://critical-art.net/?p=162.

120 Harwood, Graham, Richard Wright, and Matsuko Yokokoji. 2010. *The Social Telephony Files*. Southend-on-Sea: YoHa Limited. Accessed March 11, 2017. http://download.yoha.co.uk/social_telephony/social_telephony.pdf.

Image Credits

[Fig. 1] Critical Art Ensemble. *Molecular Invasion*. 2002. Source: http://critical-art.net/?p=1.

[Fig. 2] Critical Art Ensemble. *Molecular Invasion*. 2002. Source: http://critical-art.net/?p=1.

[Fig. 3] Parco Arte Vivente. *New Alliances*. 2012. Source: http://critical-art.net/?p=162.

[Fig. 4] Parco Arte Vivente. *New Alliances*. 2012. Source: http://critical-art.net/?p=162.

MOBILITY

INVENTION

CYCLING

STS

PATENTS

RESISTANCE

[7]

Mobile Devices of Resistance: Victorian Inventors, Women Cyclists, and Convertible Cycle Wear

Kat Jungnickel

While middle- and upper-class Victorians were quick to embrace the bicycle, cycling proved materially and ideologically challenging for women. Conventional women's fashions were vastly inappropriate for cycling: materials caught in wheels and tangled in pedals. Yet, looking too much like a cyclist in some contexts challenged established gender norms about how and in what ways women should move in and through public, to the point where cycling women suffered verbal and sometimes even physical abuse. This essay explores how some Victorians responded to challenges to women's freedom of movement by patenting

"convertible" cycle wear. These material interventions enabled women to resist social and physical limitations on their mobile bodies and identities. Drawing on feminist science and technology studies, archival research, and patents, this essay critically explores these unique garments as heterogeneous human and non-human devices and discusses how they operated as creative socio-technical mobile devices of resistance.

The craze for bicycling has made a complete revolution in the needs of dress, and there are almost as many inventions for this special amusement as days in the year. Every week at least a patent is either taken out or applied for touching on bicycle clothes. Happily there is a variety of opinion as to the requirements of this particular amusement.
The Queen: The Lady's Newspaper, 1895

This essay explores the socio-technical conditions for intervention from a historical perspective. My research is located in Victorian Britain from 1890 to 1899, which was a decade of radical social, technical, and cultural change. The Victorians are renowned for engineering and patenting, a combination of which boomed in the mid-1890s in response to the cycling craze that swept the nation. The nineteenth century brought with it mass industrialization, a plethora of new inventions, and opportunities to travel and see new worlds, which catalyzed radical ideas about what it meant to be a modern citizen. Amongst other things, out of this century came the bicycle, sewing machine, and new mass media. This essay is part of a larger project about how the Victorians responded to social, political, and technical restrictions on mobile women's bodies in public spaces. Here I discuss patented cycle wear as a creative socio-technical mobile device of resistance.

It may seem strange to readers to focus on a case study set a century before the advent of digital cultures recognizable in contemporary life. The feminist archival turn in the social sciences has opened up different ways to engage with the past in order to understand the present. Cultural studies scholar Kate Eichhorn explains how this move "has made it commonplace to understand the archive as something that is by no means bound by its traditional definition as a repository for documents" (2013, 2). Archives are a place to start, not finish, and irrespective of the time between viewer and viewed, these repositories speak to the present as much as the past. I aim to argue that there is much to learn from historic accounts of interventions, not only because past socio-technical conditions are in many ways not so different to our own, but also because they operate as useful reminders of the value of identifying and studying small, seemingly marginal, examples.

I approach the study of interventions via science and technology studies (STS). In particular I draw on actor–network theory, more commonly known as ANT, which provides a useful lens for thinking about interventions in the context of socio-technical networks. ANT emerged from early science studies in recognition of the role played by non-humans as well as humans in complex socio-technical heterogeneous networks (Law and Hassard 1999; Latour 2005). Many, including its inventors, have critiqued network theory over the years, with feminist STS scholars in particular questioning the stabilization of networks (Star 1991, 1995, 1999; Wajcman 2014). Susan Leigh Star (1991), for instance, focuses specifically on interruptions in seemingly fixed and smooth systems and processes. Her famous essay on "being allergic to onions" explores experiences that do not fit collective understandings of the world. She writes about how asking for "no onions" radically interrupted McDonald's standardized processes, resulting in a 45-minute delay to her "fast food." Simple issues like this cast heterogeneous systems in fresh light. The non-onion eating "deviant" body intervenes in the system. In doing so, it renders visible larger socio-technical systems in place, often hidden behind the scenes, that produce the standardized burger and with it the idea of a universalized consumer. These kinds of norms, Star argues, collectively "insist on annihilating our personal experience" (1991, 48). Her work reminds us that experiences, bodies, and relations to technology are much richer, more complex, and messier than this. Interventions help us see and know things differently.

Gaining these kinds of unique insights into socio-technical systems and practices, however, is not easy. Sometimes, as indicated with Star's example, it requires something to break or rupture in order to glimpse "the forgotten, the background, the frozen in place" (Star 1991, 379). They can also seem uninteresting at first. Star (1995; 1999) has done much to advocate the study of seemingly "boring" things, by pointing out that it is rarely the thing itself that is boring, but how we tend to approach it. In fact, STS scholars have argued that the more mundane and trivialized something is, the more important its role probably is in daily life. Star provides an illustrative example of how to approach the study of infrastructures, which is an often overlooked and under-valued subject of study:

> The ecology of the distributed high-tech workplace, home, or school is profoundly impacted by the relatively unstudied infrastructure that permeates all its functions. Study a city and neglect its sewers and power supplies (as many have) and you miss essential aspects of distributional justice and planning power .... Study an information system and neglect its standards, wires and settings and you miss equally essential aspects of aesthetics, justice, and change. Perhaps

and began to think of them more modestly as symbolic
sewers, this realm would open up a bit. (1999, 379)

This kind of scholarship provides ways for researchers to enter
the "black box" of socio-technical systems and practices. Black
boxes are ideas, systems or things that appear firm and fixed
after they have been in place for a while. They become familiar
and invisible; we tend to forget how they came about, what
choices were made, and which materials and processes were
accepted or rejected. Finding new ways into the black box is to
ask critical questions about their cultural, gendered, historical
and material composition. As Star writes: "When standards
change, it is easier to see the invisible work and the invisible
memberships that have anchored them in place" (1991, 44).
The crucial point here is that it is not only the technology that
becomes black boxed, but also the larger heterogeneous networks of humans and non-humans that produce and reproduce it
on a daily basis. In questioning these seemingly stable and fixed
socio-technical systems and artefacts we get to ask why we "get
the technologies we deserve" and how and in what ways they
"mirror our societies" (Bijker and Law 1992, 3).

Clothing is a particularly interesting subject for the study of
intervention. Changes in clothing portend changes in society.
Identifying, focusing and understanding these changes can reveal
much about socio-political shifts. Yet it is often overlooked and
undervalued in critical study. Barbara Burman (1999), a textile historian, has written extensively about the "culture of sewing" and
gender politics of clothing in nineteenth and twentieth century
British history. Despite the richness of this topic for understanding social shifts and gender relations she explains how
many scholars "have regarded clothing as peripheral to historical
enquiry, as too ephemeral or too everyday to warrant attention"
(1999, 3). From an STS perspective, this makes clothing a primary
area for understanding socio-technical relations.

128 My empirical focus in this chapter is on inventive forms of cycle wear, which emerged as a result of intersections of new technologies (bicycle, sewing machine, and mass media), social conditions (restrictions on women's freedom of movement), and political contexts (patenting reform, dress reform movement, and women's rights movement). How did women respond to the challenging social circumstances and physical issues presented by cycling? What did they invent? How can these inventions be seen as creative socio-technical mobile devices of resistance?

Interventions in Gender Relations and Public Space

The bicycle took Victorian society by storm in the 1890s. Although it had been around in various forms throughout the nineteenth century, it was the Safety Bicycle, with its two matching wheels, rear-drive pedaling system, lower price and easier handling that broadened its appeal and reach. While middle- and upper-class Victorians embraced this new form of mobility with enthusiasm, some found it easier than others. Cycling proved to be physically, materially, and ideologically challenging to women (Jungnickel 2015). Established Victorian social norms and behaviors for how middle- and upper-class women should move and act in public shaped how, and in many cases even if at all, they should ride a bicycle. Higher-class women were not expected to move much. At the time "leisured, or idle, wives and daughters had become expensive status symbols for successful middle-class men" (Holcombe 1973, 1). Conventional fashion, with floor-length skirts, up to seven pounds of layered petticoats, restrictive corsets, and tailored blouses and jackets, made it physically difficult if not impossible to undertake mundane domestic activities or leisure pursuits. The extent of a woman's immobility reflected the capacity she had for those around her, such as a household of servants, to be mobile. Writing about the social role of fashion, sociologist Diane Crane argues: "The ideal role of the upper-class woman, who was not expected to work either inside or outside the home, was reflected in the ornamental and impractical nature of fashionable clothing styles" (2000, 16).

The popularity of cycling in the late nineteenth century exacerbated problems with women's conventional fashion for those wishing to engage in more active lifestyles. As contemporary cyclists know, the many moving mechanisms of the bicycle do not fit well with layers of loose flapping materials. Despite this, many persisted with this unruly combination and newspapers reported on the sometimes terrible consequences.

> Sir—I see in your columns a doubt expressed as to cycle accidents due to dress. We have had a terrible one in these parts, which can clearly be traced to the skirt. I allude to the death of Miss Carr, near Colwith Force. The evidence of her friend who rode just behind her, says that "Miss Carr began the descent with her feet in the rests, but finding the hill become much steeper, she strove to regain her pedals and failed." I think she failed because she could not see the pedals, as the flapping skirt hid them from her view, and she had to fumble for them. Could she have taken but a momentary glance at their position, she would have had a good chance to save her life. The poor girl lingered a week. (The Buckman Papers 1897, *Daily Press*, September 20)

Although it had been around for a while, the dress reform movement had a resurgence in the late nineteenth century. Members campaigned on multiple platforms but broadly advocated more *rational* dress over *irrational* fashion. However, wearing more suitable cycle wear, such as rational dress in the form of bloomers or knickerbockers, short or no skirt, and looser or no corset did not result in a seamless social experience. These highly visual "New Women," who moved independently, often without a chaperone, at speed, in new places and times such as the evening, unsettled some parts of society. Their masculinized dress and behaviors were seen to "ape the lifestyles and

130 perceived privileges of manhood" (Simpson 2010, 55) and many felt society's wrath in different ways; some were denied entry to inns, catcalled in public spaces, and in some cases suffered physical violence. Writing in 1899, Irene Marshall's experience illustrates how difficult it must have been for a woman to claim a cycling identity at this time.

> But it took some courage five years ago to ride in rationals. The idea was almost entirely new and the British Public was dead against it. Hooting and screeching were then the usual accompaniments to every ride. Caps, stones, road refuse— anything was then flung at the hapless woman who dared to reveal the secret that she had two legs. And the insults were not confined to the lower classes. Well-dressed people, people who would be classed as ladies and gentlemen, frequently stopped and made rude remarks. In fact, cycling in rationals in 1894 was a very painful experience. (Marshall 1899, 40)

To cycle as a woman was an intervention in established middle- and upper-class behaviors in Victorian society. To wear radical new forms of cycle wear was yet another intervention in how a woman should move in and through public space. Neither were initially comfortable or safe positions to inhabit. While many women persisted, bravely putting their radically clothed mobile bodies in public spaces, some intervened in socio-political and technological contexts in more subtle ways through their clothing. By imagining, designing, and patenting new forms of cycle wear, such as convertible cycle wear, inventors set out to equip women with the devices to limit the possibility of harass- ment while, at the same time, resist these limitations and attempt to re-configure the parameters of conventional feminine modes of behavior and movement in public spaces.

Patents and patenting are useful sources of data for social science research. American historian of technology Ruth Schwartz-Cowan defines a patent as "a temporary monopoly on the economic benefit that can be derived from an invention. As such a patent turns an idea into a form of property; the person who has a new idea, a patent asserts, can own it in the same way that he or she may own land or money" (1997, 120). Inventors tell us about themselves, their identified problem, solution, and who in many cases they were designing for. Patents also provide a particularly good record of women's inventions, at a time when women are largely absent from other primary records.

A boom in patenting in the mid-1890s has been attributed to cycling's popularity. The late nineteenth century was a period of significant legal reform in Victorian Britain. The early 1880s Patent Reform Act greatly reduced fees and streamlined what had previously been a more complicated and time-consuming process. This opened patenting up to a wider range of new and smaller inventors. The Married Women's Property Act also came into force around this time, and allowed married women to have more control over their own property. A decade later, the cycling craze that swept the country provided further motivation for individuals to seek to claim their ideas and forge new paths into social, cultural and economic domains. Amongst patents for velocipedes and their many accoutrements were some from a group of Victorian inventors attempting to respond to the "dress problem"—how to enable women to safely and comfortably cycle while not looking too much like a cyclist. To do this, inventors intervened in what clothing could do. Many attempted to design this dual role *into* skirts:

> My invention relates to the improvements in ladies' skirts which will render them equally adapted for cyclists, tourists and ordinary wear; and has for its object to provide a skirt that will have all the comfort and convenience of a divided

skirt with a smooth seat for the saddle, and yet in walking, will be *indistinguishable from an ordinary skirt.* (Sellick 1897, emphasis mine)

This invention relates to improvements in cycling skirts and has for its object to construct these in such a manner as to allow the rider the full use of her limbs without any of the leg exposed and at the same time to *have the appearance of an ordinary walking skirt* when the rider is not on her machine. (Sibald 1897, emphasis mine)

This invention relates to improvements in connection with ladies' skirts and has for its object to provide an arrangement which can be *easily altered from an ordinary skirt* into a divided skirt and *vice versa.* (White 1897, emphasis mine)

The broad aim was to give women choice to perform multiple identities. While there were many strategies at work, I focus on a unique subset of patented cycle wear—convertible costumes. These garments enabled the wearer to convert their clothing when required, from middle- and upper-class urban walker or shopper to cyclist and back again. An illustrative example of these patented designs is by Alice-Louisa Bygrave, a dressmaker from Brixton in London. Her patent for "Improvements in Ladies' Cycling Skirts" was accepted on December 6, 1895. It features a skirt with a built-in pulley system at the front and back. Weights stitched into the hem ensured a quick change when needed. Bygrave explains her unique design:

My invention relates to improvements in ladies' cycling skirts and the object is to provide a skirt as proper for wear when either on or off the machine … I fasten a tape or cord to the bottom edge of the skirt in front and carry this cord up through suitable guides to the top of the skirt where it is made fast in any convenient way … As the wearer prepares to mount her machine, she pulls both cords in from the top, thereby raising the skirt before and behind to a sufficient height. (Bygrave 1895) [Fig. 1]

What is particularly relevant to discussions about socio-technical interventions is the location of these convertible devices in the garment. They were hidden *inside* skirts: in the seams, behind the waistbands, stitched into the hems, and hidden in gathered fabric. Concealment was central to the design. The nature of the garment would reveal itself only if and when the wearer desired it. What this also means is that the convertibility of these costumes was difficult to discern from the outside, on the surface. As evident in the larger research project in which examples of these costumes were made and worn, many of these designs only make sense on and with the body (Jungnickel 2017). This is one reason why no surviving artifacts from this period have been found (as yet) in British museums or galleries. These women did their jobs so well in deliberately concealing the nature of these garments that it makes it hard, if not impossible, to see and know the value of these designs if you are not specifically looking for them.

[Fig. 1] Illustrations of Alice-Louisa Bygrave's patented cycling skirt (Source: Bygrave 1895).

 Inventors like Alice-Louisa Bygrave recognized the desire of some women to claim multiple identities. They sought to intervene in the mobile landscape by providing wearers with choice and control. Wearers could safely and comfortably cycle if they wished. They could also choose to avoid unwelcome social abuse by not looking like a cyclist. These garments equipped women to resist dominant normative codes of behavior, at different times, and for specific purposes. Convertible cycle wear made possible *other* ways women could inhabit public space and negotiate relationships with new technologies and society.

Learnings from Historic Interventions

Why are historic accounts of interventions useful to contemporary researchers? Even though located over a century ago, these examples remind us that the past is not so far removed from the present. As Eichhorn argues, the archive should be viewed "not as a place to recover the past but rather a way to engage with some of the legacies, epistemes, and trauma pressing down on the present" (2013, 5). The history of radical new forms of mobility clothing shows us that interventions do not have to be loud, heroic, or even easy to see to produce valuable social insights. The case of convertible cycle wear is an extreme version of this. Designs were deliberately hidden, inside the seams and hems of skirts—often indiscernible to non-wearers. Yet, they intervened in the gendered normative mobile subject, making possible different means for women to negotiate mobile identities in public space at a time when this was physically and ideologically problematic. The importance of attending to marginalized or fringe behavior is also present in this essay. STS and clothing scholars argue that understanding social change comes not from a study of standardized normative behavior but rather from attending in detail to the marginalized, deviants, and rule-breakers. As Crane writes: "Had a nineteenth-century social scientist set out to predict how women would dress at the beginning of the twenty-first century, it would only have been by considering the clothing of the most marginal women in Europe and America that an accurate assessment would have been obtained" (2000, 99). Designing and wearing convertible cycle wear was not a dominant form of inventive activity, yet it is revealing for how individuals were using patents to collectively explore and materialize forms of resistance.

This research comes from the "Transmissions and Entanglements: Making, Curating and Representing Knowledge" project supported by an Economic and Social Research Council Knowledge Exchange grant with support from Intel Corporation (ES/K008048/1).

References

Bijker, Wiebe. E. and John Law, eds. 1992. *Shaping Technology/Building Society: Studies in Sociotechnical Change.* Cambridge, MA: MIT Press.

Burman, Barbara. 1999. *The Culture of Sewing: Gender, Consumption and Home Dressmaking.* Oxford/New York: Berg.

Bygrave, Alice-Louisa. 1895. Improvements in Ladies' Cycling Skirts. UK Patent 17,145 (GB189517145A). December 6, 1895. Accessed October 2, 2017. https://worldwide.espacenet.com/publicationDetails/originalDocument?CC=GB&NR=189517145-A&KC=A&FT=D&ND=3&date=18951206&DB=&locale=en_EP#.

Crane, Diana. 2000. *Fashion and Its Social Agendas: Class, Gender and Identity in Clothing.* Chicago: University of Chicago Press.

Eichhorn, Kate. 2013. *The Archival Turn in Feminism: Outrage in Order.* Philadelphia: Temple University Press.

Holcombe, Lee. 1973. *Victorian Ladies at Work.* North Haven, CT: Archon Books.

Jungnickel, Kat. 2015. "'One Needs to Be Very Brave to Stand All That': Cycling, Rational Dress and the Struggle for Citizenship in Late Nineteenth Century Britain." *Geoforum, Special Issue: Geographies of Citizenship and Everyday (Im) mobility* 64: 362–371.

Jungnickel, Kat. 2017 (forthcoming). "Making Things to Make Sense of Things: DiY as Research and Practice." In *The Routledge Companion to Media Studies & Digital Humanities,* edited by J. Sayer. London: Routledge.

Latour, Bruno. 2005. *Reassembling the Social: An Introduction to Actor-Network-Theory.* Oxford: Oxford University Press.

Law, John and John Hassard. 1999. *Actor Network Theory and After.* Oxford: Blackwell Publishers.

Marshall, Irene. 1899. *The Rational Dress Gazette, Organ of the Rational Dress League.* Correspondence, No. 10, July. p. 40. Accessed at the University of Hull.

136 Schwartz-Cowan, Ruth. 1997. "Inventors, Entrepreneurs and Engineers." In *A Social History of American Technology*, edited by Ruth Schwartz-Cowan, 119–148. New York/Oxford: Oxford University Press.

Sellick, Sebastian James. 1897. Improvements in Ladies' Skirts for Cycling and Ordinary Wear. UK Patent 780 (GB189700780A). February 27, 1897.

Sibald, John. 1897. Improvements in Cycling Skirts. UK Patent 9251 (GB189709251A). July 24, 1897.

Simpson, Clare. 2010. "Respectable Identities: New Zealand Nineteenth Century 'New Women' – on Bicycles!" *The International Journal of the History of Sport* 18 (2): 54–77.

Star, Susan Leigh. 1991. "Power, Technology and the Phenomenology of Conventions: On Being Allergic to Onions." In *Sociology of Monsters: Essays on Power, Technology and Domination*, edited by J. Law, 26–56. London: Routledge.

Star, Susan Leigh, ed. 1995. *Cultures of Computing*. Oxford/Cambridge: Wiley-Blackwell.

Star, Susan Leigh. 1999. "The Ethnography of Infrastructure." *American Behavioural Scientist* 43 (3): 377–391.

The Buckman Papers. 1894–1900. *Papers of Sydney and Maude Buckman Relating to the Rational Dress Movement and Cycling for Women*. Accessed at The Hull History Centre, UK. Ref: U DX113.

The Queen. 1895. "Dress Echoes of the Week." *The Lady's Newspaper*, 16 November.

Wajcman, Judy. 2014. *Technofeminism*. Cambridge: Polity Press.

White, Martha Kate Rose. 1897. Improvements in Ladies' Skirts, Especially Intended for Cyclists. UK Patent 11,941 (GB189711941A). June 19, 1897.

CRITICAL METHODS

POLITICIZING

AMBIVALENCES

SUSTAINABILITY

DIFFERENCES

DISCOMFORT

CONSTRUCTING ALTERNATIVES

Epilogue: Methods and Perspectives of Interventions in Digital Cultures

Martina Leeker, Tobias Schulze
and Howard Caygill

Engaging in Methods

This volume is an experiment in fostering thinking in ambivalences, which is potentially a way of dealing with the problematic constitution and situation of interventions, the facilitation of which is attempted through organization of the texts. Some essays in the book analyze the constitution of interventions, concerning either gender, history, or policy, and use the insights gained to propose various methods. Other texts focus on practices and methods of intervention in the conditions of digital cultures without specifically reflecting on the constitution of intervention itself. This combination of approaches brings about a reflection on interventions in accordance with the two aims of the book. The first aim is to examine the shaping of digital cultures by interventions, and vice versa, and the second concerns the reconciliation of the constitution of interventions in political, economic, or discursive conditions. To achieve a mutual reflection, the texts are collected under a list of methods and have been carefully balanced to enable readers' self-organized reflection on interventions.

A short reconstruction of the order and interplay of the texts, focusing on critical and reflected methods that come out of the analytical approach to interventions, should provide an insight into the power of following, and thinking in, interventions' ambivalences.

Reading the Chapters

Fred Turner proposes *historicizing* as a method for exploring the aesthetics and dramaturgies of interventions in today's digital cultures. In his interview, Fred Turner talks about the multi-screen environments that were used in the 1940s/1950s and the 1960s as an aesthetic means to develop what he calls the "democratic surround." The aim of the surround was the creation and control of self-determined, democratic individuals by training them to form their own worldview by piecing together fragments. But even as the artists involved were trying to achieve an emancipative social arrangement, they became part of a Cold War policy of forced democratization and, furthermore, engaged themselves in attempts to control the effect of this process. This context is to be taken on board as a prehistory of today's digital cultures as well as interventions into them. In this framework, a historical approach clarifies the instrumentalization of interventions, or of art as intervention, in order to understand which methods, concepts, and dramaturgies we should avoid repeating. The aim is securing interventions against a repetition of this history. Instead of intervening in digital cultures by immersion in multisensory environments as affective and cognitive apparatuses and happenings of unconscious Be-In, Fred Turner votes for the establishing of distances and differences. An example is the photographic work of Wayne Lawrence (2013) at Orchard Beach, the Bronx Riviera, which presents people at respectful close-range. It is about standing still, according to Fred

Turner, about looking and reflecting, instead of—in accordance
with the analysis of this problematic status of interventions—
acting and performing. This is one possible method against the
big techno-ecological players today, involving people immersively
in socio-technological systems.

Howard Caygill also follows a historical reconstruction of interventions in digital cultures and at the same time stands for
research into its ambivalent political constitution. He refers to
Clausewitz's notion of resistance in the sense of the capacity
to survive violent attacks (*Widerstandsfähigkeit*), using, for
example, secrecy as a strategy. The prehistory of interventions
in Clausewitz's concepts of secrecy and resistance shows that
as a form of resistance in digital cultures, interventions can
apply equally to war as to subversion, freedom, and equality.
This strategic constitution also conditioned the configuration
of the Internet by Paul Baran within the RAND Corporation in
the late 1950s and early 1960s, creating an Internet that is able
to survive attacks by being decentralized and, at the same time,
creating secrecy by using cryptography. A genealogical point
of view excavates the paradoxical constitution of the Internet,
determining today's resistance to and interventions in it. The
appropriate method for interventions is *thinking in ambivalences*.
Fighting against the state's monopolizing of information
technologies also means fighting against decentralization. Intervening in digital cultures has to be sensitive to the paradoxical
situation, grounding itself firstly in decentralized structures in
order to not leave traces. It could, secondly, use encryption,
knowing that this calls the state's resistance investigating in
strategical cryptography. Interventions in digital cultures ask
for continuous reflecting, keeping the military and war contexts of resistance in mind and pondering the interplay of the
opponents, each envisaging its own survival. Howard Caygill's
contribution provides training to think about the ambivalences of
interventions.

 Alexander R. Galloway also opts for intervention in infrastructures. He claims the invention and realization of other infrastructures in the manner of *other*, so-called ad hoc *networking*, which could, in reference to Howard Caygill, enable invisible interventions in moments of revolution. Instead of interrupting infrastructures and software in interventions as hackers did in the 1960s, Alexander R. Galloway argues that today, we need robustly running alternatives.

Making differences and enabling discomfort are the methods Wendy Hui Kyong Chun proposes for interventions in digital cultures, especially in their infrastructures as networks and databases, working against homophily and habits that constitute them. Habits build infrastructures and survive even technological or social changes. Homophily, a concept from 1950s' sociology meaning love of the same, generates heavy segregation as a basic constitution of, for example, social networks. Against this background, Wendy Hui Kyong Chun calls for the establishment of critical digital humanities that become indispensable in digital cultures, in which Big Data analysis or user profiling are done by ideologically based, recursive algorithms. Overcoming the prejudices concerning gender, race, and class, as well as habits that all together constitute data processing, requires the invention of other infrastructures as interventions in digital cultures, and for that, transdisciplinary cooperation is necessary.

Ulrike Bergermann also votes for the power of differences and differentiation as a basis for interventions in digital cultures. In her example, she explores the human microphone as a medium of protest, which she studies in terms of a *critical politicizing of space*. The affordance of this analog medium in interventions in digital cultures is not to speak for the other. A gendered being-with should help to overcome prejudices and pre-inscriptions in collective protest, which can exclude those who should have a voice in protesting. For interventions in digital cultures, questions of the politics of space, leading to those of gender and race, need to be clearly in focus. Both Ulrike Bergermann and Wendy Hui

Kyong Chun highlight that it is not technology itself that can bring critical points to digital cultures, but the concepts they are based on.

Steve Kurtz also stresses the importance of differences as a basis for continuous interventionist work. He gives an overview of the intervention methods and projects of the Critical Art Ensemble (CAE), which has been active since 1987. They carry out interventions into destructive ecological situations, biotechnology, and digital technology. In every field, the intervention methods are *interrupting* and *queering* in order to make people think differently, and *speculating* to find alternative ways. These methods overcome the problematic hype about pure performativity, also mentioned in Fred Turner's insight into the history of interventions, and transform interventions into a work of continuous queering as an institution of critically dealing with digital cultures.

Kat Jungnickel confirms the importance of continuity for effective and non-violent interventions with an example from the nineteenth century. She discusses a subversive strategy that enabled women to ride bikes in the strict and normative Victorian age. A skirt with a concealed option to transform into a trouser-like garment, freeing women to be mobile; challenging violence with viscosity, which resulted in sustainable changes. Referring to Howard Caygill's analysis of the ambivalences of resistance, the women performed a *calm*, continuous, intelligent and *sustainable* revolution that could be taken as a model of interventions in digital cultures.

Outlook: Differences, Discomfort, Sustainability

The interplay of contributions to this volume reveals a common call for interventions capable of introducing differences

144 concerning racial, gender, or political inscriptions on the level of technology, concepts, habits, and thinking (see McPherson 2012).

It has also yielded a second result that is just as important. Instead of following the hype about never-ending performative intervening, it is an affirmation of calm and sustainable interventions (see Kat Jungnickel), and the building of alternative and sustainable infrastructures (Alexander R. Galloway) that will be effective and productive. Now, just when digital cultures have become part of everyday life, interventions seem less invested in interruption, which used to be the primary aesthetic, and more invested in construction and building. At the same time, as it becomes obvious in Steve Kurtz's interview, there is still a need for pranks, subversion, stumbling blocks, and thus methods, aesthetics and dramaturgies for enabling a permanent and sustainable indicating of problems and strengthening of attention and perception, as well as rethinking in order to follow critical and problematic progressions in the current and future development of digital cultures.

References

Lawrence, Wayne. 2013. *Orchard Beach: The Bronx Riviera*. Munich: Prestel.

McPherson, Tara. 2012. Why Are the Digital Humanities So White? or Thinking the Histories of Race and Computation. Accessed March 29, 2017. http://dhdebates. gc.cuny.edu/debates/text/29.

Authors

Ulrike Bergermann is Professor of Media Studies at the Art University Braunschweig, Germany. Her research interests include the histories of academic disciplines, and post-colonial and gender studies.

Howard Caygill is Professor of Modern European Philosophy at Kingston University, London. His research interests are in the fields of the history of philosophy, aesthetics, and cultural history. He is the author of several books, including Walter Benjamin: *The Colour of Experience* (1998), *Levinas and the Political* (2002), *On Resistance: A Philosophy of Defiance* (2013), and the forthcoming *Kafka: In Light of the Accident* (2017).

Wendy Hui Kyong Chun is Professor of Modern Culture and Media at Brown University, Rhode Island. She has studied both systems design engineering and English literature. She is the author of *Control and Freedom: Power and Paranoia in the Age of Fiber Optics* (MIT Press, 2006), *Programmed Visions: Software and Memory* (MIT Press 2011), and *Updating to Remain the Same: Habitual New Media* (MIT Press 2016).

Alexander R. Galloway is author or co-author of seven books, most recently a monograph on the work of François Laruelle titled *Laruelle: Against the Digital* (Minnesota, 2014). He teaches media theory at New York University.

Kat Jungnickel is a Senior Lecturer in the Sociology Department at Goldsmiths, University of London. She is the author of *DiY WiFi: Re-imagining Connectivity* (Palgrave Macmillan 2014) and the soon to be published *The First Wheelwomen: Cycling, Sewing and Suffrage* (Goldsmiths Press/MIT Press).

Steve Kurtz, Ph.D., Professor Emeritus, is a founding member of the interventionist art and theater group Critical Art Ensemble. Founded in 1987, this collective of artists of various specializations—including digital imaging and web design, wetware, film/video, photography, text art, book art, and performance—is dedicated to exploring the intersections between art, technology, political activism, and critical theory.

Martina Leeker is Professor of Methods in Digital Cultures and Senior Researcher at the Digital Cultures Research Lab, Leuphana University Lüneburg, Germany. Her research interests include art and technology, critique in digital cultures, systems engineering and infrastructures, theater and media, and critical media theory. She undertakes practical artistic research in discourse-analytic aesthetics: "Fragile Queering and Critical Speculation."

Tobias Schulze is a masters student in media studies at Humboldt University Berlin, a research assistant at the Digital Cultures Research Lab, Leuphana University Lüneburg, and a tutor at Hochschule für Bildende Künste Braunschweig. His focus in work and studies is on entanglements between art, temporality, and media.

Fred Turner is the Harry and Norman Chandler Professor in Communication at Stanford University, California. He is the author of several books on media and American culture since World War II, including *From Counterculture to Cyberculture* (2006) and most recently, *The Democratic Surround: Multimedia and American Liberalism from World War II to the Psychedelic Sixties* (2013).